Dostoevsky: A Very Short Introduction

T0021767

VERY SHORT INTRODUCTIONS are for anyone wanting a stimulating and accessible way into a new subject. They are written by experts, and have been translated into more than 45 different languages.

The series began in 1995, and now covers a wide variety of topics in every discipline. The VSI library currently contains over 750 volumes—a Very Short Introduction to everything from Psychology and Philosophy of Science to American History and Relativity—and continues to grow in every subject area.

Very Short Introductions available now:

Available soon:

For more information visit our website

www.oup.com/vsi/

Deborah Martinsen

DOSTOEVSKY

A Very Short Introduction

OXFORD
UNIVERSITY PRESS

OXFORD
UNIVERSITY PRESS

Great Clarendon Street, Oxford, OX2 6DP,
United Kingdom

Oxford University Press is a department of the University of Oxford.
It furthers the University's objective of excellence in research, scholarship,
and education by publishing worldwide. Oxford is a registered trade mark of
Oxford University Press in the UK and in certain other countries

Published in the United States of America by Oxford University Press
198 Madison Avenue, New York, NY 10016, United States of America

British Library Cataloguing in Publication Data
Data available

Library of Congress Control Number: 2023943565

ISBN 978-0-19-886433-2

Printed by Integrated Books International, United States of America

Contents

Preface

Reading Dostoevsky can be a life-changing experience. With his concerns for the big questions, revolutionary narrative technique, and insights into human nature, Dostoevsky plunges us into the action of his texts and into the minds of his characters. He creates sympathy for an envious, paranoid bureaucrat who fears he is losing his mind (*The Double*), and for a philosophizing shame-driven misanthrope (*Notes from Underground*). He makes most of us root for an axe-murderer fleeing the scene of his crime (*Crime and Punishment*). He discomfits us by drawing uncomfortable parallels between a fallen woman and a fallen general (*The Idiot*). He distresses us by exploring the issue of suicide (*Crime and Punishment, Idiot, Demons, Diary of a Writer, The Brothers Karamazov*). He provokes us by treating metaphysical questions with humour (*The Brothers Karamazov*). He makes us wince with shame at witnessing others' shame. In short, Dostoevsky provides awe-inspiring depth and breadth of vicarious experience. Finally, Dostoevsky affects us at both ends of the spectrum. On one hand, he so unnerves some readers that they put down his work, never to pick it up again. On the other, he inspires some to study Russian and become Russian studies scholars. Mostly Dostoevsky motivates us to read more Dostoevsky.

Deborah Martinsen, 2021

The six chapters of this book each focus on a major theme and a major work. Chapter 1 gives the story of Dostoevsky's dramatic life, situating it within the journalistic politics of his time and introducing his semi-autobiographical, topical, and non-fictional writing, notably *Notes from the Dead House* and the *Diary of a Writer*. Chapter 2 introduces the important theme of psychological and philosophical duality that figures centrally through Dostoevsky's writing, beginning with *The Double*. Chapter 3 examines the complex, 'dialogic' first-person narrative structure of *Notes from Underground* and its philosophical implications. In Chapter 4, an analysis of geography, space, and setting anchors the discussion of Dostoevsky's treatment of social justice themes in *Crime and Punishment*, opening out into an analysis of scandal scenes in threshold spaces. Aesthetics and ethics in two novels written abroad, *The Idiot* and *Demons*, is the focus of Chapter 5. The book culminates in a deep dive into Dostoevsky's famous 'eternal questions' as addressed in his last novel, *The Brothers Karamazov*. At the end of each chapter the analysis expands outward, showing linkages to other works. Throughout the book, a master theme of shame and guilt is shown to be at work in Dostoevsky's writing, contributing to its enduring psychological and emotional power.

Deborah Martinsen wrote this book during the last two years of her life after a distinguished career as a world-renowned scholar and beloved teacher and colleague. Her major academic works, which underlie her unique approach to Dostoevsky, are listed under 'Further reading', along with other classics of criticism. Over the past two years, many colleagues were able to read and share their comments on chapters-in-progress with the author, including Randall Butler, Ellen Chances, Paul Contino, Nicole Fermon, Andrew Kahn, Ron Meyer, Marcia Morris, Savannah Pearson, Amy Ronner, Jennifer White, and myself. Deborah was able to incorporate many of these contributions in the book, which we are now honoured to share with you on her behalf.

Carol Apollonio,
2023

List of illustrations

Note on translation, citation, dates

All citations from Dostoevsky's work are from the academic edition of the *Polnoe sobranie sochinenii v tridstati tomakh* (Leningrad: Nauka, 1972–90, volumes 1–30). All translations are mine unless otherwise indicated. When citing a work of fiction, I include the part or book number and chapter number so that readers can find the passage in whichever translation they are using. The opening page of *Crime and Punishment*, for example, would be cited as (Pt I, ch. 1). All italicized words in quotations are italicized in the original unless otherwise indicated.

All citations from Dostoevsky's letters will be referenced by date of letter or date of letter and addressee. Citations from the *Diary of a Writer* (*DW*) and notebooks are given by month and year. All Russian dates are given in accordance with the Julian (Old Style) calendar used in Russia before 1917. In the 19th century, it was 12 days behind the Gregorian calendar used in the West. For sources quoted from the West, both dates are given.

I use a dual system of transliteration for Cyrillic names, following the guidelines in J. Thomas Shaw's Transliteration of Modern Russian for English-Language Publications. In the text and in all discursive parts of the references, I use Shaw's 'System I'. This system Anglicizes Russian proper names: the 'y'-ending is used instead of 'ii'; 'yu'/'ya' is used instead of 'iu'/'ia'; 'oy' is used instead of 'oi'; 'x' replaces 'ks', etc. However, 'ai' and 'ei' are used at the end of names instead of 'ay' and 'ey' (Andrei, Nikolai, Sergei). Well-known spellings are used for famous people (e.g. Peter the Great). When citing Russian sources in the bibliography and references, I use the Library of Congress system without diacritics (Shaw's 'System II').

Dostoevsky

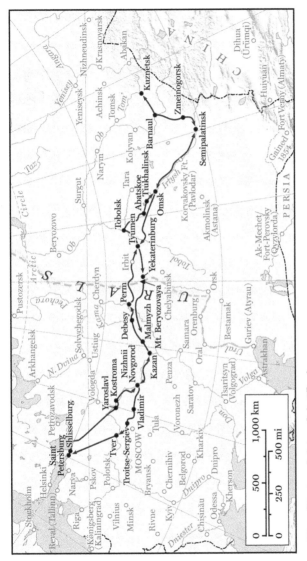

1. Map of Dostoevsky's travels in Siberia.

Chapter 1
Dostoevsky's dramatic life and writing: *Notes from the Dead House* and the *Diary of a Writer*

When he was 33, Fyodor Mikhailovich Dostoevsky (1821–81) characterized himself as 'a child of the century—a child of disbelief and doubt' with a terrible 'thirst for faith' (January–February 1854 letter to N. D. Fonvizina). This ability to hold opposite positions while exploring each extreme may have roots in Dostoevsky's dramatic life and times. Born in Moscow in 1821 shortly before the reign of Nicholas I (1825–55), Dostoevsky died in St Petersburg in 1881, six weeks before Alexander II was assassinated. Under Nicholas I, whose repressive regime controlled political thought and crushed dissent with restrictive policies on all facets of life, Dostoevsky was arrested, incarcerated, and exiled to Siberia. Under Alexander II, whose more liberal government initiated the Great Reforms needed to modernize Russia, Dostoevsky was allowed to return to St Petersburg, participate in the era's lively journalistic debates, and write the novels that made him famous. This chapter contextualizes Dostoevsky's life and works within their time, first offering a brief biographical sketch, then addressing his non-fictional and journalistic writing, which influences and interacts with his fiction in important ways and has left a problematic legacy that continues into the 21st century.

A writer's life

The second son of seven children, Fyodor Dostoevsky was raised on the grounds of the Mariinsky Hospital for the Poor in Moscow, where his father, a former army surgeon, worked as a doctor. After his mother died when he was 16, Fyodor's father sent him and his older brother Mikhail to St Petersburg, where Fyodor attended the Academy of Engineers. He was thus living in Mikhailovsky Castle, the building where Tsar Paul I was murdered, when he learned of his father's sudden death. At the time there were rumours that he had been murdered by his own peasants; these rumours have never been substantiated, but they most certainly affected Dostoevsky's thinking; the seeds of the parricide/regicide/deicide theme in *The Brothers Karamazov* can be seen here. As an engineering student, Dostoevsky excelled at drawing and spent much time reading. Although physically slight, he nevertheless protected vulnerable classmates from hazing. Dostoevsky graduated in 1843 as a lieutenant, served briefly as a military engineer, and quickly resigned his commission to devote himself to writing.

When Dostoevsky finished writing his epistolary novella *Poor Folk* in spring 1845, he gained overnight fame and enjoyed a brief season of celebrity. When *The Double* was published in January 1846, Dostoevsky was criticized for abandoning social themes and fell into disrepute. In 1847, he met the utopian socialist Mikhail Butashevich-Petrashevsky and joined his discussion circle. In 1848, as revolutions broke out throughout Europe, Dostoevsky joined a secret society within the Petrashevsky Circle led by the charismatic revolutionary Nikolai Speshnev. In 1849, Dostoevsky was arrested for reading aloud a banned letter at a Petrashevsky Circle meeting, incarcerated in the Peter-Paul military fortress for nine months, and condemned to death by firing squad. Awaiting execution in Semenovsky Square, Dostoevsky stood hooded with the second group of three scheduled to be shot. He turned to his companion Speshnev and said, '*Nous serons avec le Christ*' (We'll be with Christ), to which Speshnev replied that they would be dust. A moment later, following Nicholas I's cruel script, a drumroll resounded and the firing squad lowered their rifles, ending the sadistic mock execution and inspiring the end-of-life motif that runs through much of Dostoevsky's subsequent writing.

Dostoevsky's death sentence was commuted to four years of hard labour (1850–4) and exile in Siberia (see Figure 1). As a political convict, he lived and worked in leg-irons in a Siberian stockade in Omsk, sharing close quarters with a multi-ethnic, largely illiterate group of peasant criminals from all reaches of the Russian Empire. Dostoevsky was shocked by the cruelty of corporal punishment and the social divide between the educated and the peasants, who considered men like him part of the oppressing class. On top of the crowding and stench, Dostoevsky suffered intellectual privation: he had constant access to only one book—the New Testament—although he was occasionally able to read Dickens during periods when he was in the hospital (see Figure 2). Once released from prison, he served five years as a soldier in Semipalatinsk, where he met Maria Isaeva, whom he would marry in Kuznetsk in 1857. Although Dostoevsky was first diagnosed and treated in the 1840s for epilepsy, an illness that figures in both *The Idiot* (Prince Myshkin) and *The Brothers Karamazov* (Smerdyakov), he petitioned to return to St Petersburg by claiming his seizures began during his incarceration.

In 1859, Dostoevsky returned to St Petersburg and resumed his literary career (see Figure 3). Arriving just before the serfs were liberated, he witnessed the unravelling of the social evil that had prompted him to join the Petrashevsky Circle and its radical wing. For the rest of his life Dostoevsky sympathized with radicals' aspirations for social improvement, but saw revolutionaries as truth-seekers and self-sacrificers gone astray. Post-Siberia, he wrote novels criticizing the ideas that drove revolutionaries' actions, including *Crime and Punishment* and *Demons*. In this era

ГОСПОДА НАШЕГО

ІИСУСА ХРИСТА

НОВЫЙ ЗАВѢТЪ.

Цѣна въ переплетѣ 2 руб. 25 коп.

Первымъ изданіемъ.

САНКТПЕТЕРБУРГЪ.
Въ Типографіи Россійскаго Библейскаго Общества.
1823.

2. Dostoevsky's prison New Testament title page.

3. Dostoevsky in 1861.

of reform, Dostoevsky travelled abroad, enjoyed newly liberalized censorship policies, and, most importantly, participated in the exciting public debates raging in Russia's increasingly vocal print media.

Fyodor and his brother Mikhail eagerly joined the polemical fray, launching two journals: *Time* (1861–3) and *Epoch* (1864–5). Although Fyodor's name was not displayed on the masthead because he was a former political prisoner, he served as the managing editor for both journals. He also provided editorials, ideological direction, and major works of fiction for them, including his semi-autobiographical novel *Notes from the Dead House* (1860–2), which re-established his reputation as a great humanitarian writer, as well as his travelogue *Winter Notes on Summer Impressions* (1863) and his polemical novella *Notes from Underground* (1864). *Time* was suppressed by the government in May 1863. When the Dostoevsky brothers finally got permission to open a new journal in November, the usual subscription season had passed, and the new journal *Epoch* began its life in January 1864 with shaky finances. The 1864 deaths of Dostoevsky's first wife Maria and his brother Mikhail left Dostoevsky struggling to carry on *Epoch*, which closed in March 1865.

Burdened by the journals' debts, plus the care of his brother's family and his wife's son, Dostoevsky went on an unsuccessful gambling spree in Europe. In September 1865, a desperate Dostoevsky turned to Mikhail Katkov, the editor of the journal *Russian Herald* and his former ideological rival, to pitch his idea for *Crime and Punishment*. Although Dostoevsky was anxious about approaching him, Katkov was a pragmatic editor and his journal needed good writers. He sent an advance. When *Crime and Punishment* began serialization in 1866, it was an instant success. Dostoevsky subsequently published *The Idiot* (1868), *Demons* (1871–2), and *The Brothers Karamazov* (1879–80) in the *Russian Herald*.

In October 1866, while serializing *Crime and Punishment*, Dostoevsky took a month's break in order to write *The Gambler*, an extraordinary novella about gambling addiction written while Dostoevsky was still a gambling addict. In order to meet the strict deadline required to retain the rights to his published work, including *Crime and Punishment*, Dostoevsky hired a young stenographer, Anna Grigorievna Snitkina. Shortly after meeting the deadline, Dostoevsky took another gamble and proposed to Anna. They moved to Europe after their marriage to escape his creditors (see Figure 4).

During the next four years (1867–71), the Dostoevskys moved often. In 1867, they spent several months in Baden-Baden, the gambling resort where Dostoevsky famously quarrelled with his fellow novelist Ivan Turgenev (1818–83), then moved to Geneva, where their first daughter Sophia was born and where, after three short months, she died (1868). The heartbroken pair moved to Vevey and then to Florence, where Dostoevsky finished *The Idiot*. They next moved to Dresden, where their daughter Lyubov was born in 1869. That year, after reading about a student murdered by the revolutionary Sergei Nechaev and his co-conspirators, Dostoevsky began work on *Demons*. The serialization of *Demons* began in 1871, the year the Dostoevskys returned to Petersburg, where their son Fyodor was born.

While Dostoevsky's journals of the 1860s (*Time*, 1861–3; *Epoch*, 1864–5) staked out a middle ground between journals on the right and those on the left, by the late 1860s there was no middle ground. *Demons'* anti-nihilistic stance garnered Dostoevsky the reputation of a conservative. As a result, in 1873, Dostoevsky re-entered the journalistic world as editor of *The Citizen*, a weekly periodical published by the conservative Prince Vladimir Meshchersky. There Dostoevsky began his *Diary of a Writer* as a column. In 1874, burdened by editorial work and a contentious relationship with his publisher, Dostoevsky quit the weekly to write *The Adolescent*, which began serialization in the liberal

4. Anna Grigorievna Dostoevskaya, Dostoevsky's second wife.

journal *Fatherland Notes* in 1875, the year the Dostoevskys' son
Alexei was born. Dostoevsky then returned to journalism as sole
writer, editor, and publisher of the monthly *Diary of a Writer*
(*DW*, 1876–7, 1880, 1881). *DW*'s multi-voiced narration allowed

readers to project their own positions onto its contents, so the journal enjoyed wide popularity with readers across the political spectrum. In the December 1877 issue, Dostoevsky announced that he was taking a break from *DW* to start what would be his last novel—*The Brothers Karamazov*.

In May 1878, after Alexei (aged 3) died suddenly of an epileptic seizure, Dostoevsky, along with the young philosopher Vladimir Solovyov, visited the Optina Pustyn monastery to seek an audience with the elder Amvrosy, who became a prototype for Zosima in *The Brothers Karamazov*. Dostoevsky's final novel confirmed his national reputation and later secured his international fame. From the depths of prison under Nicholas I, Dostoevsky thus rose to the heights of fame under Alexander II. His funeral in February 1881 was a major public event, with thousands attending.

Facts and the fantastic: Dostoevsky the journalist in the 1860s

Unlike his wealthy contemporaries Ivan Turgenev (1818–84) and Lev Tolstoy (1819–1910), Dostoevsky lived exclusively by his pen. Journalism provided income, but, more importantly, it allowed Dostoevsky to immerse himself in the burning issues of his day. Current events and the forces and ideologies behind them were the fodder for his fiction. We can thus look at his journalism as Dostoevsky's fact-gathering laboratory.

Dostoevsky understood the necessity for immersion in issues of the day: in an 1867 letter written from Geneva to his niece Sofya Ivanovna, he wrote of the necessity 'to be at home and to see and hear everything with my own eyes' (Letter of 29 September 1867/11 October 1867). While still abroad, Dostoevsky wrote to his colleague Nikolai Strakhov:

> I have my own view on reality (in art), and that which the majority calls almost fantastic and exceptional is sometimes the very essence

of the real for me. Everyday phenomena and the conventional view of them are not, in my opinion, realism but even the opposite. In every newspaper you find report of facts that are very real and yet very strange. To our writers they seem fantastic, and they do not deal with them; and yet they are real because they are *facts*. Who is going to notice them, explain and write about them? They occur by the minute and every day; they are not *exceptional*.

(Letter of 26 February/10 March 1869)

Dostoevsky's view of reality thus derived from print media—if an incident appeared in print, he considered it a fact to explore. In his February 1876 *DW*, he writes, 'A novelist could never imagine possibilities such as real life offers every day by the thousands under the guise of the most ordinary things.' Dostoevsky aimed to get to the heart of the facts, to grasp the reality behind them, to go deeper into the mysteries of personality that produced them. Even as a 17-year-old, Dostoevsky wrote to his brother Mikhail, 'The human being is a mystery. The mystery must be solved, and if you work at solving it all your life, don't say that you have wasted your time. I occupy myself with this mystery because I wish to be a human being' (Letter of 16 August 1839). This early allegiance to human psychology sets the tone for all his subsequent writing.

Dostoevsky's return to St Petersburg in 1859 coincided with relaxed censorship and Russia's first period of *glasnost'* (openness). Consequently, new print media proliferated. Given the Russian government's strict control over public discourse, political thinking had moved into literature and criticism, which found their home in the 'thick journals'. These were monthly compendia of literary, philosophical, economic, political, scientific, and journalistic content. Journals were thus sites of education and cultural formation as well as ideological partisanship and contention. Most 19th-century Russian novels, including all of Dostoevsky's, were first published serially in journals, as was the case in England with Dickens, for example.

As the 1860s progressed, newspapers competed for readership, but in 1860, when the Dostoevsky brothers advertised their new journal *Time*, journals were still the major players. To attract readers, the Dostoevsky brothers positioned themselves between the more conservative Slavophiles, who pursued national renewal in Russian institutions (especially the peasant commune), and the increasingly radicalized heirs to the Westernizers, who criticized Russia's backwardness and advocated secularism and science. Before *Time* was shuttered by the government in 1863, both camps were enthusiastic about the reforms being enacted, and Dostoevsky polemicized with ideological opponents in both camps. Along with his talented colleagues Apollon Grigoriev and Nikolai Strakhov, Dostoevsky articulated and promoted the doctrine of *pochvennichestvo* (an ideology of Russianness rooted in the soil), which advocated closing the gap between the largely Western-educated classes, most of whom had become alienated from the Russian soil, and the masses of uneducated Russians.

Notes from the Dead House

Years in prison and exile deepened Dostoevsky's understanding of the huge gulf between educated and uneducated Russians. The gap not only became the touchstone of *Time*'s editorial position, but remained a constant in Dostoevsky's work. It is most starkly seen in his *Notes from the Dead House*, which combined autobiography, fiction, and documentary. As readers knew, it drew from Dostoevsky's own experiences like an autobiography or documentary, yet it was structured like a novel with both a fictional narrator and a fictional editor.

While Dostoevsky may have had one eye on the censor as he distanced himself from the narrator of *Dead House*, he had already begun speaking in another's voice as early as *Poor Folk*. Writing to his brother Mikhail, he explained that his characters speak for themselves: readers 'do not understand how it is possible to write in such a style. They are used to seeing the author's mug in everything; I don't show mine. It never occurs to them that it's Devushkin speaking, and not I, and that Devushkin cannot speak any other way' (Letter of 1 February 1846). In *Dead House,* Dostoevsky creates a persona—the narrator Goryanchikov, imprisoned for murdering his wife—and largely speaks from that voice. Years later he creates another persona, the *DW* writer—and does the same. Occasionally, however, the lines between author and narrator blur, and readers discern Dostoevsky's voice behind his narrative mask. This blurring, the sense of closeness to an author who has lived through such hardship, is part of the appeal of Dostoevsky's journalistic work. For clarity's sake, I will use 'Dostoevsky' only when referring to the authorial voice behind the persona.

Throughout *Dead House,* Dostoevsky's educated narrator Goryanchikov repeatedly stresses his alienation from the peasant convicts around him. In Part I, for example, he notes, 'everywhere I was out of place' (Pt I, ch. 6). In Part II, when Goryanchikov learns that the convicts have gathered to protest the prison food, he offers to join them but is rebuffed as an outsider: 'what kind of companion are you to us?' his bewildered addressee replies (Pt II, ch. 7). Behind such emblematic incidents illustrating the great social and educational divide, we hear the voice of Dostoevsky. Thus, when Goryanchikov observes, 'no matter how fair-minded, good-natured and intelligent' a nobleman is, the convicts will despise, misunderstand, and, most importantly, 'not trust him' (Pt II, ch. 7), readers rightly detect the life experience of Dostoevsky himself. Such moments of leakage articulate the gap between the educated and non-educated prisoners in a very personal way. This gap between elite and peasantry, both in his personal life as well as in Russia as a whole, will continue to preoccupy Dostoevsky, and he will return to it often in his fictional and journalistic writing.

Dead House also documents moments of rapprochement and communion between the educated and non-educated prisoners.

A strong advocate of literacy and education for the masses (a tenet of *pochvennichestvo*), Dostoevsky includes an episode in which Goryanchikov teaches the young Daghestan Tatar Alei to read. This practical approach to bridging the gap anticipated the 1870s Populist movement, when young people went to the countryside to educate peasants. There, to their surprise and consternation, these fervent young reformers met the same kind of suspicion and hostility Dostoevsky/Goryanchikov had.

More rapprochement occurred during holidays—Christmas, followed by the convict theatrical, and Easter, attending church and receiving alms. Here Dostoevsky highlights the themes of memory and community that resonate in the rest of his work. As the convicts prepare for Christmas, Goryanchikov observes, 'The days of the great feasts are sharply imprinted on the memory of the common people, beginning in childhood' and 'In addition to his inborn sense of reverence for the great day, each convict unconsciously felt that by observing this feast he was in some way coming into contact with the whole world, that he was not altogether an outcast, a lost man, a severed limb' (Pt I, ch. 10). The community outside the prison brings food for the convicts, which the prison cooks distribute equitably. And while Christmas Day produces great anticipation and elaborate preparations, it largely ends with drunkenness and disappointment. The same is not true for the Christmas theatrical.

The Christmas show was a convict-initiated enterprise that engendered collective excitement. In recognition of his greater knowledge and experience of the theatre, Goryanchikov is seated by the convicts near the front of the crowded barracks, an honour he attributes to the people's 'sense of justice and their thirst for it' (Pt I, ch. 11). He realizes that they do not suffer from the desire to be first in all things, whether they deserve it or not, and observes:

> One has only to remove the outer, superficial husk and look at the
> kernel within more attentively, more closely and without prejudice,

and one will see in the common people things one had no inkling of. There is not much that our men of learning can teach the common people. I would even say the reverse: it is they who should take a few lessons from the common people.   (Pt I, ch. 11)

In this commentary, we hear Dostoevsky's doctrine of *pochvennichestvo*, with its emphasis on communion between the educated and the uneducated classes. The commentary also stresses the importance of perspective, which is characteristic of Dostoevsky's oeuvre. Shortly after this moment, Dostoevsky decries the waste of vigour and talent caused by imprisonment (Pt I, ch. 11). He points to the transformation such a collaborative change from prison routine can make: 'All that was needed was for these poor men to be allowed to live in their own way for a bit, to enjoy themselves like human beings, to escape from their convict existence for an hour or so—and each individual underwent a moral transformation, even if it only lasted for a few minutes…' (Pt I, ch. 11). Again we hear Dostoevsky's voice supporting creative communal activity as a means of transforming prisoners' lives. In contrast to the holiday party, which ended in drunkenness, this collective theatre experience encouraged collaboration among the prisoners and rapprochement between the educated and uneducated, however short-lived.

Although less saliently, Dostoevsky continued portraying the great divide between educated and uneducated Russians throughout his work—often, but not always, in gendered contexts. In *Crime and Punishment*, the landlady's servant Nastasya shares her own tea with Raskolnikov and reminds him of her murdered friend Lizaveta. Sonya, Marmeladov's daughter, has little education but knows her Gospels. In the prehistory of *Demons*, Stepan Verkhovensky gambles away his serf Fedya, who murders the Lebyadkins in the novel. In *The Adolescent*, the great class divide is highlighted both by the rift embodied in the illegitimate first-person narrator, the son of a peasant mother and an educated father, and by the rift between his biological father Versilov and his nominative father, the holy peasant Makar Dolgoruky. In *The Brothers Karamazov*, Fyodor Pavlovich is murdered by his servant and presumed illegitimate son Smerdyakov. In these instances, Dostoevsky highlights attempts to overcome the class divide in everyday social relationships, often presenting them in microcosm in broken families—or what is known as the 'accidental family' theme in his work.

In *Dead House*, Dostoevsky embeds social justice commentary while describing the prison. The novel not only documents the deprivation of freedom and forced labour, but the torment of 'compulsory communal cohabitation' (Pt I, ch. 2). The crowded, mephitic barracks were tormenting. In the deliberately Dantesque bathhouse scene, convicts are crammed into a steamy inferno, where there was 'not a space the size of a man's palm on which convicts were not sitting huddled' (Pt I, ch. 9).There, densely packed men on shelves used birch switches to lash themselves 'into a state of intoxication'. 'This whole mass of men was shouting and howling to the accompaniment of a hundred chains dragging on the floor.' There, 'The shaved heads and the steaming red bodies of the convicts seemed more grotesque than ever. When the convicts' backs are steamed like this, the scars previously left by whips and sticks stand out distinctly, so that all these backs now looked as though they had been newly wounded. What horrifying scars!' (Pt I, ch. 9). Such vivid descriptions help explain why *Dead House* prompted a huge journalistic debate about the Russian justice system and prisons.

Dostoevsky's writing was indelibly marked by his time in Siberia. Incarcerated for his desire to end serfdom, he met with hostility from the peasant criminals whose close quarters he shared. He lived first-hand the danger of what he was to describe as 'ideas floating in the air' and the power of an idea to seduce a young mind towards violence. Later, in *DW* (February 1876), he writes about the powerful impact of positive memories that sustained him during his imprisonment, citing an incident from his

5. Monument to Dostoevsky in Tobolsk, Siberia, site of the transit prison where he received his New Testament from the Decembrist wives in 1850.

childhood when his fear of a wolf was soothed by the peasant Marei—a name that calls to mind Mary, the mother of God. Seeing his fear, Marei stroked young Dostoevsky's cheek, blessing him—'Christ be with you'—and encouraging him to cross himself. When Marei saw that young Fyodor was still trembling, he reached out his 'earth-soiled' finger and touched the boy's lips to calm him. In this passage, and throughout his post-Siberian writing, Dostoevsky writes as a man torn from the soil, who recovers his connection to the people through a positive memory of physical and spiritual contact (Figure 5).

The 1870s: *Diary of a Writer*

Dostoevsky's journalism was thus a two-way street: his non-fictional writing provided material for his fiction, and his fiction focused attention on contemporary social justice issues. Dostoevsky's

1870s journalism covered many of the same issues as that of the 1860s: court reforms and the legal profession, the relationship of the educated classes to the Russian people, and generational conflict. However, in the 1870s, Dostoevsky increasingly worried about the fragmentation of society, and he added articles on suicide, contemporary youth and 'accidental families', Russia's relationship to the West, and the Balkan War. His writings on suicide and court cases particularly illuminate the deep links between his journalism and fiction.

Suicide

Dostoevsky considered suicide a metaphysical, moral, and social issue, and it haunts *DW* and his oeuvre. In *Crime and Punishment*, for example, Dostoevsky envisioned suicide as one alternative for Raskolnikov, who instead chooses to follow Sonya's directive that he bow down at the crossroads to kiss the earth and confess his crime. In *The Idiot*, the consumptive Ippolit attempts suicide during the birthday party for Prince Myshkin. In *Demons*, Stavrogin and the young girl he rapes both hang themselves. In *The Brothers Karamazov*, Dmitry contemplates suicide, and Smerdyakov dies by suicide.

Throughout his work, Dostoevsky worried about the alienation of the educated classes from the Russian soil. He was convinced that such alienation was responsible for many suicides. Dostoevsky's *DW* writer (1876–7) devotes much attention to suicides, including ideological suicides that he believes result from an 'inflexible' view of life: 'The Russian land seems to have lost the capacity to hold people on it,' he writes in the May 1876 issue of *DW* (Pt II, ch. 2). He sees such suicides as children of their age, suffering from rational disbelief while thirsting for some higher ideal in which to believe, capable of self-sacrifice for a society from which they are wilfully alienated. *DW*'s frequent articles and stories concerning suicide articulate the journal's values, which are couched as oppositions: alienation vs rootedness in the soil; intellect vs belief;

dissociation vs community; indifference vs living life; inflexibility vs complexity; simplification vs contextualization; and complacency vs anxiety. 'A Gentle Creature' (*DW*, November 1876) offers a notable treatment of the theme that incorporates religious imagery. On the psychological, social, political, and metaphysical levels, these oppositions reflect the dominant underlying metaphor of separation and union.

The narrator from Dostoevsky's story 'Dream of a Ridiculous Man' (April 1877), *DW*'s last piece of fiction, embodies all of the aforementioned oppositions. His rationalism and indifference, symptoms of his psychic and social alienation, lead him to contemplate suicide. His dream not only saves him from suicide but dramatizes Dostoevsky's oft-repeated conviction that belief in God leads to love of life. In the story, the reintegration of the anonymous narrator's psyche leads to love for the earth: 'I cried out, shaking from an incontrollable, ecstatic love for that former native earth that I had cast off' (ch. 3). Personal reintegration also leads to love for others: 'I love everyone, those who laugh at me more than all the others' (ch. 5). His indifference and complacency give way to passionate involvement in life and a burning sense of mission: he seeks out a despairing little girl whom he had earlier driven away because she had interrupted his suicide. The dream integrates his mind and heart, restoring him to the earth and human community by releasing his positive emotional energy—his active love for others.

By offering readers a fictional story of conversion—from alienation and isolation to love and community—the 'Dream' exemplifies the *DW* writer's rhetorical tactic of providing exemplars. The *DW* writer also employs many real-life models, including the peasant Marei, who comforted young Dostoevsky when he feared that he had heard a wolf (February 1876); the nanny who offered his mother her life savings when the Dostoevsky estate burned down (April 1876); Foma Danilov, a Russian soldier martyred for his faith (January 1877); women who have devoted themselves to the common cause (May 1876) or shown their sacred qualities during the war with the Turks (September 1877); and Pushkin, Russia's national poet, who displayed unparalleled universality (August 1880). *DW*'s most ideal figure is Christ, the incarnate God (discussed in Chapter 6).

Court cases

Court cases provided a natural subject for Dostoevsky—they were topical and sensational. In the 1860s, *Time* and *Epoch* joined the heated press debates over court reforms. In the 1870s, as political trials (which could not be discussed in public) proliferated, journalists transferred their attention to criminal trials and the role of lawyers. Dostoevsky's coverage of three trials in particular—the Sayapin case (1873), the Kroneberg case (1876), and the Kornilova case (1876–7)—illustrate his interest in the issue of broken families. They also form a progression that reveals Dostoevsky's moral agenda. These cases all touch on the emotionally charged issues of wife-beating or child abuse. Each involves a family of three—man, woman, and child. In each, a stronger figure abuses a weaker one; the abused are all female; and the aggressors act deliberately. The *DW* writer examines both the particulars of each case and the verdicts' impact on society. He proceeds dialogically, first personifying his opponents' moral positions, then demolishing their rhetoric by recontextualizing, appealing to images and emotions, and proposing alternatives.

One of the first articles Dostoevsky wrote for his 1873 *DW* was devoted to the newly instituted system of trial by jury. Entitled 'The Environment', the article addresses the issues of determinism and misplaced compassion by embodying them as the rhetorical standpoints of an imaginary lawyer and an actual jury. The article begins by discussing the English concepts of citizenship and court systems and by appealing to jurors' civic responsibility. The *DW* writer deftly summarizes the Sayapin case: 'Most simply put, a woman hanged herself as a result of her husband's beatings;

the husband was tried and found deserving of leniency' (8 January). The *DW* writer attacks the lawyer's appeal to the 'environment' defence, that is, that crime results from injustices built into social institutions, making criminals victims of society. The *DW* writer counters this defence by highlighting the issue of personal responsibility.

The *DW* writer engages readers' emotions by dramatizing the family scene, leaving us with the unforgettable image of a peasant beating his wife. Given the portrayed brutality, the peasant commune's response to the wife's plea for help—that she 'Go, live in peace'—reads as a strong condemnation of the patriarchal status quo. They see that Sayapin's wife is battered, but they assume that she is responsible for her abuse. The *DW* writer praises the jury's natural compassion, that is, their identification with the abuser, but points to the consequences of this false compassion, that is, their reluctance to ruin another person's life. In embracing false assumptions, the peasant jury perpetuates the cruelty. The *DW* writer imagines the effects of the father's cruelty on the daughter, who starves with her mother, trembles in the corner as her mother is beaten, and discovers her mother's hanged body. Since the jury's leniency means only eight months of incarceration for the father, the *DW* writer speculates that, upon his release, Sayapin will demand his daughter's return, and the cycle of violence will continue: 'There will again be someone to hang by the feet.' Leniency for the father spells probable death for the daughter. The jury's compassion is myopic.

Dostoevsky's January 1876 issue of *DW* introduces the themes of children, family, and education that will recur throughout *DW*'s next two years and resurface in *The Brothers Karamazov*. He then devotes the greater part of his February 1876 issue to discussing the Kroneberg case. Kroneberg severely beat his 7-year-old daughter with a cat-o'-nine-tails until the peasant concierge threatened to call the police. After seeing the child's bruised body, she reported him. Spasovich, a famous attorney, defends his client by downplaying the beating's severity, portraying it as pedagogy gone awry. The *DW* writer focuses on the young child's suffering. Claiming to write about the case because he intuits moral falsity, he introduces themes he develops here and elsewhere in *DW*: thoughts vs emotions, the letter vs the spirit of the law, parental authority vs love, and, in an Aesopian text, government vs people.

Whereas Spasovich assumes the role of dispassionate investigator and employs legal, scientific language to distance his audience from sympathy for the child, the *DW* writer counters by adopting the child's perspective. Whereas Spasovich treats her as a child who wilfully flouts parental authority, the *DW* writer tells the story of a lonely, abandoned child, full of the desire to please and be loved. Whereas Spasovich tries to deny the extent of the child's physical suffering, the *DW* writer amplifies it by pointing to her physical injury and psychological suffering. Whereas Spasovich argues that the relationship between father and child is analogous to that between a state and its citizens, the *DW* writer advocates relationships based on reciprocal love. He closes by appealing to compassion, which he claims is an inherent characteristic of the Russian people and which he presents as a model for social interaction. Since he has associated compassion with peasant women like the concierge, he again illustrates the divide between educated Russians and the people.

In both the Sayapin and the Kroneberg cases, the *DW* writer appeals to readers' compassion for weak and defenceless women and children against powerful men (fathers, husbands, lawyers). He prepares his defence of Kornilova, a wife, by entitling his first article on her 'A Simple, but Complex Case'. Kornilova, 20 years old and pregnant, in a fit of anger at her husband, pushed her 6-year-old stepdaughter out of a fourth-floor window. The child miraculously survived. Struck by the strangeness of the case, Dostoevsky called for an in-depth investigation (May 1876). After her trial and sentence to almost three years' hard labour, followed by permanent exile to Siberia, Dostoevsky wrote a lengthy article

(October 1876), which led directly to the case being reviewed and resulted in Kornilova's acquittal. His May 1877 article announcing her return home drew fire from a journalistic opponent, who accused him of defending a child abuser. Dostoevsky strategically withheld return fire until the concluding article of his December 1877 issue of *DW*.

In justifying his defence of Kornilova, the *DW* writer resorts to many of the same rhetorical strategies for which he had earlier condemned his lawyer opponents: shifting the readers'/jury's attention away from the abused child; ignoring or marginalizing the child's trauma; creating sympathy for the abuser; and invoking an outside force as cause. He grounds his defence of Kornilova (and thus himself) in the affect rising from pregnancy; the consequences of her sentence (probable prostitution) and its impact on her and her unborn/newborn child; her immediate self-surrender to police; the short-sightedness of simplifying the case; and the beneficial effects of social compassion on the Kornilov family and society itself. Though his appeal to post-partum depression smacks of the positivist discourse he decries elsewhere, the *DW* writer emphasizes Kornilova's self-surrender as the conclusive proof that her crime was unpremeditated, not an act of systematic child abuse.

The *DW* writer's position in each case depends on the voluntary or involuntary nature of the act, the defendant's motives, the family's fate, the consequences for the community, his own moral intuitions, and, most critically, the defendant's sense of personal responsibility. In his view, Sayapin was completely unrepentant; Kroneberg capable of repentance; and Kornilova fully repentant. Kornilova's self-surrender thus proves her worthiness for mercy. The Kornilova case also demonstrates how Dostoevsky exploited serial publication to his own ends. In May 1876, he calls attention to the case; in October 1876, he argues for mercy; in May 1877, he announces her release, and in December 1877, he triumphantly argues that the seed of mercy had fallen on good ground and that

Kornilova had been reborn into the community. Here, as elsewhere, the *Diary* writer refers to his earlier articles and then reports the fulfilment or explains the disconfirmation of his earlier predictions, thereby confirming his status as prophet.

Devils

Although Dostoevsky is known for treating serious social and metaphysical issues, he is also a self-consciously playful writer. One *DW* article that displays his wit and anticipates issues dramatized in *The Brothers Karamazov* is entitled 'Spiritualism. Something about Devils. The Extraordinary Cleverness of Devils, If Only These Are Devils' (January 1876, ch. 3.2). Citing reports of dancing chairs and devils, the *DW* writer mocks the current craze for séances and spiritualism. The phenomenon had become so widespread that a Committee of Inquiry into Spiritualism, which included the famous scientist Dmitry Mendeleev, was formed.

First, the *DW* writer calls the committee incompetent, arguing that for it to succeed, it would need at least one member who would admit the hypothetical existence of devils. He then notes that the committee, as composed, will most likely deny the devils' existence. Moreover, if the committee recommends that practitioners be restricted or persecuted, spiritism will spread like wildfire: 'Mystical ideas love persecution; they are created by it' (January 1876, ch. 3.2).

Next, the *DW* writer claims that even though he does not believe in devils, he has devised a strong proof of their existence. He introduces others' voices: 'people write that spirits are stupid (by spirits I mean devils, the Unclean Power, for other than devils, what spirits can be at work here?)' (January 1876, ch. 3.2). He counters with a question—what would happen if the devils displayed their powers? He answers that devils could reveal discoveries that would allow humankind to provide for all of its material needs; in short, they could realize the Russian socialists' dream. He follows with a counter-argument: quickly people would see that they had lost their freedom, their will, their personality, that 'their lives had been taken away for the sake of bread, for "stones turned into bread"' (January 1876, ch. 3.2). People would realize that there is no happiness in inactivity, that the mind which does not labour will wither, that it is not possible to love one's neighbour without sacrificing something to him of one's own labour, that it is vile to live at the expense of another, and that '*happiness lies not in happiness but only in the attempt to achieve it*' (January 1876, ch. 3.2). Mass suicides would ensue. The remaining people would then cry out to God: '"Thou art right, O Lord: man does not live by bread alone!" Then they would rise up against the devils' (January 1876, ch. 3.2).

The *DW* writer thus adduces the current controversy as the greatest proof of the devils' existence. Albeit tongue in cheek, this article anticipates Ivan Karamazov's Grand Inquisitor, who accuses Christ of giving human beings too much free will and instead offers 'miracle, mystery, and authority'—the satisfaction of material needs and political absolutism clothed in religious garb. The article also prepares for Ivan Karamazov's devil, who professes to sow belief with seeds of doubt. Finally, the *DW* writer concludes that devils are astute politicians, who operate by sowing the seeds of discord. The very fact of the committee proves it. No matter what it decides, the devils will have a heyday.

Russian nationalism

While Dostoevsky displays keen insight on social issues, when he turns to contemporary politics, he uses his own vociferous Russian nationalism to engender *DW*'s most strident vitriol. The *DW* writer treated the issue of Russia and the West in an extremely personal and novelistic manner as a conflict of personalities. He characterized Russia, France, and Germany as embodiments of their national spirits, defined by their religious roots: Catholic France, Protestant Germany, Orthodox Russia. Tracing Russia's social ills to European influence on the educated classes, the *DW* writer argues that all political forms produced by Europe—the Catholic Church, the French Republic, socialism, and Protestantism—descend from the Roman Empire with its doctrine of conquest and temporal power. By contrast, the *DW* writer maintains that Russia's spiritual health and future lies with the Russian people, who, despite their poverty, backwardness, corruption, and drunkenness, have preserved both their belief in Christ and their sense of community. Once the people and the educated classes unite (which he saw happening in the Balkan War), Russia, the repository of true Christianity, would offer universal salvation. Despite its ugly chauvinism, Dostoevsky's nationalism was immensely appealing to Russian readers in its day, and, alas, in ours.

Dostoevsky's belief that orthodox Russia would save the world effected a critical change in *DW*'s composition. From 1873 to January 1876, and from December 1876 to December 1877, the *DW* writer gradually shifted his position: instead of presenting issues from multiple perspectives and voices, he increasingly adopted a single, strident, prophetic voice. Yet in its coverage of social issues and in its initial multiplicity of voices and perspectives, *DW* served as a laboratory for his last novel, *The Brothers Karamazov*. There he dramatically portrayed the reunion of a

Dostoevsky's nationalism: a note from the editor

The author of this book did not live to witness the Russian invasion of Ukraine on 24 February 2022 and thus was unable to address it in the text. While we cannot speak in her voice, we do feel that she would want her readers to understand how Dostoevsky's nationalism has contributed to a toxic and militaristic version of 'the Russian idea' that some cite to justify Russia's war in Ukraine.

Carol Apollonio, 2023

broken family, its fatal consequences, and one of the most famous trial scenes in literary history.

Dostoevsky's enduring relevance

Dostoevsky's writing was always relevant and never uncontroversial; his views on Russian nationalism and pan-Slavic unity remain disturbing and relevant. But it is his writings on universally human questions that continue to reach readers in a changing world. Like Dostoevsky, we are living in a period of crisis and transition. His concern with such issues as social justice, women's rights, prisons, the court system, suicide, free will, belief, the power of ideas, the need for community, and freedom of the press thus resonates with us. Dostoevsky continues to engage readers emotionally as well as intellectually in ethical, social, and metaphysical issues that have remained urgent to this day.

Chapter 2
Duality and doubles:
The Double

The protagonist of *The Double* (*Dvoinik*), Dostoevsky's second published work (1846), haunted the writer. He recognized the novella's significance as the place where his 'underground type' originated, and he revised the novel in 1866, and revisited it in 1877. Returning from his Siberian exile, Dostoevsky wrote to his brother Mikhail, 'Why should I lose a first-rate idea, a character type of supreme social importance that I was the first to discover and of whom I was the herald?' (1 October 1859). In one of his 1870s notebooks, he called his protagonist Golyadkin 'my most important underground type' (Notebook 6 for *DW*). And in his November 1877 *DW*, Dostoevsky proclaimed, 'I never advanced anything in literature more serious than this idea.' We will thus begin with *The Double*, not only because of its seminal importance, but also because it bears the hallmarks of Dostoevsky's best writing: psychological depth, narrative experimentation, and universality.

Although Dostoevsky's contemporaries praised his first novella, *Poor Folk* (written and circulated spring 1845), for depicting the poor and downtrodden, they condemned *The Double* (published January 1846) for being wordy and fantastic. Yet like all of Dostoevsky's work, *The Double* was both a product of its time and a harbinger of things to come. Doubles were a commonplace in 1830s and 1840s literature (in works by E. T. A. Hoffman and

Edgar Allan Poe for example), but Dostoevsky's *The Double* became *the* case study. Jane Austen and Gustave Flaubert had already employed free indirect discourse (character speech conveyed without quotation marks) to convey characters' thoughts, but Dostoevsky mixed direct speech (quoted utterances) and indirect speech long before it became a common strategy in the early 20th century (in works by Virginia Woolf and Franz Kafka, for example). In addition, although Alexander Pushkin and Nikolai Gogol had established a strong foundation for Russian literary writings about St Petersburg, the Russian literary tradition of the Petersburg text, Dostoevsky cemented it with *The Double* and *Crime and Punishment*. Finally, Dostoevsky recognized that exploring doubleness was a source of creative intensity—not just an expression of good versus evil or simple binaries, but of the multiplicity and complexity of being. Dostoevsky was thus very much a part of, but also ahead of, his time in his use of literary techniques, mastery of genre, and character complexity.

A plot of dissociation and shame

The Double recounts the events of four days in the life of an ambitious, mid-level—civil service rank nine—middle-aged bureaucrat. The story opens as Mr Golyadkin prepares to skip work and attend the name-day party of State Councillor—civil service rank five—Olsufy Ivanovich Berendeev's daughter Klara, whom he unrealistically aspires to marry. He hires a carriage, rents livery for his servant, and drives along Nevsky Prospect, Petersburg's major thoroughfare, immortalized by Gogol as a symbol of Petersburg's duality—beautiful façades covering moral corruption. Yet, as encounters with his fellow clerks and superior Andrei Filippovich reveal, Mr Golyadkin's desire to be seen by others matches his desire to hide from them. Dostoevsky thus provides an early clue about the role of shame in Mr Golyadkin's story. Shame is about our identity and involves seeing and being seen. On one hand, Mr Golyadkin associates being seen with power, a sign that he is an agent in control, recognized and admired by others. On the other, he associates being seen with being exposed, vulnerable, objectified, and diminished by others. Three times in the first three chapters, Mr Golyadkin defends his exposed self with a powerful gaze 'calculated to reduce his foes to ashes'. In chapter 4, he loses the ability to conjure up this protective gaze and falls back on his other defences—dissociation and self-objectification. As early as chapter 1, Mr Golyadkin sees his fellow clerks on the street and mutters, 'Why, what's so strange in that? A man in a carriage, a man needs to be in a carriage, so he hires a carriage.' After his superior catches sight of him, Mr Golyadkin huddles in the carriage's corner and mutters to himself, 'It's not me, it's not me.' This practice of dissociation helps prepare readers for Mr Golyadkin's ultimate self-objectification—the encounter with his double.

Mr Golyadkin meets his double in chapter 5 on a deliberately clichéd dark and stormy November night, after fleeing Klara's name-day party, which he had crashed. On one of Petersburg's iconic twin bridges, Mr Golyadkin first senses, then sees, and finally recognizes his double. Five chapters later, his double publicly humiliates him, and the memory haunts Mr Golyadkin's sleep. Here is part of Mr Golyadkin's dream (ch. 10, revised version, 1866) recounted by Dostoevsky's narrator:

> Beside himself with shame and despair, the ruined but perfectly legitimate Mr Golyadkin fled blindly wherever fate might lead. But with every step, with every thud of his foot on the granite of the pavement, there leaped up, as though from under the earth, an exact, perfectly alike Mr Golyadkin with a repulsively depraved heart. And all these perfect likenesses immediately upon appearing began to run one after the other, stretching out in a long chain, like a file of geese, waddling after Mr Golyadkin Senior, so that there was nowhere to escape from these perfect likenesses,—so that Mr Golyadkin, most worthy of pity, was breathless with horror,—so that finally there multiplied a

terrifying host of perfect likenesses,—so that finally the entire
capital was overflowing with perfect likenesses, and a policeman,
seeing such a disruption of decorum, had to grab all these perfect
likenesses by the scruff of the neck and throw them into a police
booth that happened to be nearby...Frozen and numb from
horror, our hero was awakening, and frozen and numb from
horror, was feeling that his waking time was hardly more
cheerful...It was oppressive, tormenting...Such anguish
overcame him, it was as though someone had gnawed the heart
from his breast...   (ch. 10)

In this final part of Mr Golyadkin's night-long angst-ridden
dream, Dostoevsky uses the vivid imagery of proliferating
likenesses to dramatize Mr Golyadkin's sense of unending shame
and horror. By using the biblical word 'likeness' (*podobnyi*) in this
passage, Dostoevsky adds a deviant religious dimension,
reminding readers that we are all created in God's image and
'likeness'. By having every step of Mr Golyadkin's blind flight
produce yet another perverted 'likeness', Dostoevsky's narrator
poignantly identifies Mr Golyadkin as their source. By adopting
Mr Golyadkin's perspective ('the ruined but perfectly legitimate
Golyadkin'), the narrator reveals the way Mr Golyadkin projects
his own ambition—experienced as a 'repulsively depraved
heart'—onto the endless chain of evil Golyadkins. Finally,
Dostoevsky's narrator intensifies Mr Golyadkin's sense of anguish
by combining the comic with the horrific. By using climaxing
verbal and symbolic repetitions in this dream, Dostoevsky's
narrator amplifies Mr Golyadkin's anguish, which has intensified
since the first day he sees his double at his office (ch. 6).

The policeman's offended sense of decorum emphasizes
Mr Golyadkin's self-division and the dream's shame content.
By projecting his shameful ambition onto myriad pursuing
doubles, Mr Golyadkin splits himself into persecutors and
persecuted. Mr Golyadkin's numb horror derives from the
unexpected and disorienting experience of shame, which

undermines an individual's sense of self and place in the world. The passive nature of the shame experience and its attendant self-consciousness reinforce his tormenting anguish. From the outset of his story, Mr Golyadkin has been acutely conscious of decorum (*prilichie*, literally, the presence of face). He objects to his fellow clerk calling out to him from the street, and he worries whether it's proper to drop by his doctor's office unannounced (ch. 1). By having a lone policeman single-handedly grab and thrust this capital, full of indecorous geese, into a comically small space, Dostoevsky reveals how Mr Golyadkin's own divided psyche both produces and represses the threat from within. Throughout his story, Mr Golyadkin exercises the standard defences against shame—denial and flight: he repeatedly asserts 'It's not me' (it is), 'I'm all right' (he's not), 'I'm not an intriguer' (he is), and he repeatedly flees the scenes of his shame. When he awakens from this dream, he vows to engage in the less socially accepted defence against shame—aggressively passing his shame on. In a comic vein, the narrator quotes a letter that Mr Golyadkin writes to the other Mr Golyadkin that starts with a challenge—'My dear sir, Yakov Petrovich! Either you or I, but both together is impossible'—and ends with a challenge—'I lay down my pen and wait... However, I am ready to be at your service and—to pistols' (ch. 10). Here as elsewhere, Mr Golyadkin engages in double-think with his double—blaming him for existing.

Duality and doubles

Repetition as narrative strategy

Dostoevsky exhibits his literary mastery by inscribing Mr Golyadkin's repetition compulsion into his novella through a series of doublings. Here and elsewhere, Mr Golyadkin flees shame. Twice he is seen in his carriage and shrinks into its corner (ch. 1). Twice he shakes his double's hand, only to be humiliated by him (chs 10, 13). Twice Mr Golyadkin takes a carriage to the Berendeevs' house to seek a one-sided meeting with Klara (chs 3, 12). Twice Mr Golyadkin dismisses his carriage and spends two hours huddled in small spaces waiting for his moment to act. Twice Mr Golyadkin becomes the focus of attention for being out of place (chs 4, 13).

The story's repetitions mark the progression of Mr Golyadkin's social exclusion, geographical marginalization, and psychological disintegration. Mr Golyadkin's desire to be seen repeatedly leads him to expose himself; he is then humiliated, flees, regroups, reasserts himself, and is again humiliated. Surprised by shame, Mr Golyadkin becomes disoriented and excessively self-conscious. He responds by denial and flight. Yet Mr Golyadkin compulsively repeats the pattern. When he crashes the party in chapter 4, Klara screams; the orchestra stops; all eyes fix on Mr Golyadkin as he is escorted from the house. The clock ominously strikes midnight. As he flees, the narrator notes: 'Mr Golyadkin did not only want to run away from himself, but to be obliterated, to cease being, to return to dust' (ch. 5). From the ashes of his humiliation, however, his double arises. As he hurries home to seek refuge from the Berendeevs', a place he does not belong, Mr Golyadkin encounters a familiar figure, who turns out to be 'none other than he himself,—Mr Golyadkin himself, a different Mr Golyadkin, but absolutely the same as he himself,—in a word, what is called a double in all respects' (ch. 5). The narrator closes this chapter with a whole line of periods, as if to emphasize the horror of the recognition.

Mr Golyadkin crashes Klara's name-day party—a place he does not belong—and flees from shame. He then repeats the pattern, at home and at work, until he again oversteps the bounds of the socially permissible—he deludes himself into believing that Klara wants to elope with him. As in the earlier incident, Mr Golyadkin shows up to a party uninvited, once again violating a social taboo. In chapter 13, he goes to the Berendeevs', but sits outside in the courtyard behind a woodpile waiting for Klara to join him. Suddenly, as he waits outside, all eyes fix on him 'from every window'. This moment represents the culmination of his social exclusion, geographical marginalization, and psychological disintegration. He is brought inside, where Dr Rutenspitz waits for him, only to accompany him, presumably to the mad house. Mr Golyadkin thus starts and ends his adventures in a carriage, initially as actor, finally as one acted upon. The presence of Dr Rutenspitz at the beginning and end of the story brings the narrative full circle.

Dostoevsky uses verbal repetitions, biblical language, and compassion mixed with satire to accentuate Mr Golyadkin's identity crisis. In his dream, the phrase 'perfect likenesses', repeated five times, underscores Mr Golyadkin's horror of doubling and thus losing his self. At the same time, the phrase's biblical language reminds readers both that Mr Golyadkin is one of God's creations and that Mr Golyadkin's 'likenesses' are also creations—his own and Dostoevsky's. Mr Golyadkin's most frequent verbal mantras focus on his identity and betray his duality: 'I'm my own person' (*ya sam po sebe*), 'like everyone else' (*kak i vse*); 'I'm all right' (*ya nichego*, literally I'm nothing); 'I'm not an intriguer' (*ya ne intrigant*); and 'I'm not a rag' (*ya ne vetoshka*). The first two—'I'm my own person' and 'like everyone else'—are often used together. These repeated self-assurances—different yet same—have a double edge: like everyone, Mr Golyadkin wants to be seen as an individual with agency and self-worth (different), but he also wants to be like people who fit in (same). More particularly, he wants to be recognized and valued by his superiors and accepted into their corrupt company. The sense of Mr Golyadkin's anguish over these conflicting desires is intensified for readers in the dream passage when Dostoevsky uses escalating anaphora—repeating the phrases 'so that' (3×); 'finally' (3×); 'but with' (2×); 'frozen and numb from horror' (2×). Dostoevsky also mixes compassion for Mr Golyadkin's anguish and horror with the humorous repetition of his frequent double locutions like 'such and such' (*tak i tak*). Finally, the repeated phrase 'perfect likenesses' highlights Mr Golyadkin's anxiety about exposure—his dark underside. His naked ambition has not only emerged 'as though from under the earth', but it has replicated for all to see. By this point in his story, his darkness not only emanates from him; he cannot keep it in check.

The Double as Petersburg text

Like all Dostoevsky's fictions, *The Double* is a drama of identity. Fittingly, it is enacted in Petersburg, a city with dual identities. Peter the Great's 'Venice of the North' is both Russian and European, a granite city constructed on a swampy delta and a modern city whose grand façades concealed its seamy undersides. Peter himself was seen as world creator and Antichrist, and his city came to symbolize the tensions between God and the devil, culture and nature, authoritarian government and long-suffering people. *The Double* offers a taste of how Dostoevsky exploits Petersburg's topography by using city sites to signal Mr Golyadkin's ambition and self-division. Mr Golyadkin lives on Shestilavochnyi Street, in a neighbourhood populated by mid-level bureaucrats, yet fantasizes about marrying Klara and moving to the Izmailovsky Bridge neighbourhood, home to upper-level bureaucrats. His two unwelcome visits to the Berendeevs (crashing the party from the inside and waiting outside behind a woodpile) dramatize both his social ambition and his intense guilt for desiring to overstep social and moral boundaries. Dostoevsky may end Mr Golyadkin's story tragically, but he satirically exposes the comedy of Mr Golyadkin's aspiration to achieve the status and perquisites of his corrupt bureaucratic superiors. Like Peter's city, Mr Golyadkin is defined by his own duality.

While Dostoevsky's novella is psychologically compelling, it is also delightfully self-conscious of its literary construction. The repeated 'thud' of Mr Golyadkin's fleeing steps on the granite pavement recalls Evgenii, the poor clerk who flees from the animated statue of Peter the Great in Pushkin's narrative poem (*poema*)

The Bronze Horseman. The Pushkinian intertext is underscored by
the subtitle—*Petersburg Poem* (*poema*)—which Dostoevsky
adopted for his 1866 revision. His original subtitle—*The
Adventures of Mr Golyadkin*—more limitedly evokes Gogol's novel
Dead Souls, also subtitled *poema* (despite being written in prose),
and the travels of its rogue hero Chichikov, who schemes to
advance himself socially. The revised subtitle clearly evokes and
emphasizes the city of Petersburg, its ubiquitous founder Peter,
Pushkin's Petersburg texts *The Bronze Horseman* and 'The Queen
of Spades', and the theme of madness.

Like the Petersburg texts of Pushkin (particularly *The Bronze
Horseman* and 'The Queen of Spades') and Gogol (particularly
'The Nose'), Dostoevsky's *Double* creates epistemic uncertainty by
blurring the boundaries between the real and the fantastic as well
as between the narrator and the character. Does Mr Golyadkin's
double exist or doesn't he? Like its predecessors, Dostoevsky's
novella offers evidence for a both/and rather than an either/or
reading. Dostoevsky builds on his predecessors' work by
inscribing authorial insights into psychological characterization,
thematic exploration, and narrative strategy. Mr Golyadkin has
boundary problems, manifest in his inability to distinguish where
reality ends and paranoid fantasy begins. Accordingly,
Dostoevsky's narrator blurs the boundaries between himself and
Mr Golyadkin by going in and out of his hero's head, frequently
slipping from indirect discourse to external narrative voice by
using Mr Golyadkin's verbal mantras—'I'm my own person', 'like
everyone else', 'I'm all right'—and his verbal tics—'so they say',
'such and such', 'this and that', and 'it may all work out for the
best'. Of Golyadkin's magic gaze, which had the power 'to reduce
his enemies to ashes', the narrator writes: 'this gaze completely
expressed Mr Golyadkin's independence, that is, it said clearly
that Mr Golyadkin was completely all right, that he was his own
person, like everyone else' (ch. 2). While 20th-century readers
like Nabokov delighted in this complex modern form of

narration, Dostoevsky's narrative experiments unsettled contemporary readers accustomed to clear boundaries between characters and narrators.

Doubling, impostorship, and counterfeiting

Dostoevsky further exhibits his literary mastery by embedding the novella's themes of exposure, doubling, and deception into Mr Golyadkin's names. Mr Golyadkin's last name comes from the word 'golyi' (naked) and thus expresses his sense of being exposed. His first name Yakov suggests the biblical twin Jacob, the younger son who cunningly cheats his brother Esau of his birthright. Fittingly, in Dostoevsky's novella, Mr Golyadkin's double uses his social cunning to usurp his elder's position. Mr Golyadkin's patronymic Petrovich (literally, 'son of Peter') marks his relationship to Peter the Great, in whose extensive bureaucracy he and his double serve. The novella's 13 chapters recall the apostle Judas, the 13th guest who betrayed Jesus at the Last Supper: Mr Golyadkin's double not only repeatedly betrays him, he gives him a 'Judas kiss' in chapter 13. Finally, the theme of impostorship evokes a long tradition in Russian history, which witnessed numerous popular uprisings led by men, such as the 'false' Dmitrys, pretending to be the 'true' tsar.

Dostoevsky's treatment of these themes also reflects the early 19th-century Russian monetary system, which, as Gillian Porter notes, was plagued by unwanted doubles. The 1839–43 financial reforms, designed to eliminate the differences between the silver and paper money standards caused by widespread counterfeiting, actually highlighted the instability of Russian currency. In chapter 3, Mr Golyadkin changes his large bills for smaller ones, increasing the size of his wad, but decreasing its value. Dostoevsky designates these bills *assignatsii*, the old name for paper money, but he describes *kreditnye bilety*, the new, multi-coloured bills. By underscoring the discrepancy between the name stated and the thing named, he accentuates

Names in Russian

On first encounter, Russian names appear bewildering, but once you know the system behind naming in Russian it becomes much easier to keep track of who's who.

All names in Russian consist of three components. For the sake of illustration, let's look at the names of our writer, Fyodor Mikhailovich Dostoevsky, and his wife, Anna Grigorievna Dostoevskaya. First comes the given name (Fyodor, Anna); followed by the patronymic (Mikhailovich, Grigorievna), which is formed from the father's given name and the suffix -ovich or -evich (for men) and -ovna or -evna (for women); then comes the surname, which often has masculine and feminine forms as well (Dostoevsky; Dostoevskaya).

Most given names also have diminutive or affectionate forms. Let's look at Rodion Romanovich Raskolnikov, the protagonist in *Crime and Punishment*, and his sister Avdotya Romanovna Raskolnikovna. Raskolnikov's mother and sister affectionately address him as 'Rodya', the diminutive form of Rodion. His friend Razumikhin calls him 'Rodka'. The diminutives in these cases are easy to decipher, but not all diminutives are quite so easy to recognize. For example, the diminutives for Avdotya are Dunya and Dunechka. Fortunately, English translations of Dostoevsky's fiction often include a list of characters' names.

How a character is addressed can convey important information about both speaker and addressee. The reader will notice that characters are routinely addressed by first name and patronymic together (without surname), which connotes some degree of formality, often when in English we would use Mr, Mrs, or Ms. For example, Rodion always addresses the investigator as Porfiry Petrovich (in fact we never learn his surname). Porfiry Petrovich addresses Raskolnikov first as Rodion Romanovich (Part IV), and later as Rodion Romanych (Part VI)—the clipped ending of the patronymic suggests a degree of familiarity.

Box credit: Ronald Meyer

the novella's epistemological uncertainty. Just as paper money is unstable, so are Mr Golyadkin's words: he issues a number of false promises, leading others to call him a counterfeiter of speech. Yet the greatest threat to Mr Golyadkin's reputation comes from his double, whom both the narrator and Mr Golyadkin describe in the language of counterfeiting (*fal'shivyi*/false and *poddel'nyi*/counterfeit). Dostoevsky also deploys a graphic doubling when Mr Golyadkin eats one pastry in a café, and the cashier charges him for 11. Mr Golyadkin wonders whether there's sorcery going on until he sees his double in the doorway, realizes he has found the culprit, and calls him a counterfeiter. Dostoevsky's play on monetary and linguistic counterfeiting thus highlights the novella's theme of impostorship, emphasizes the thin line between the true and the false characteristic of Petersburg texts, and prepares for its return in *Demons* (1871).

The Double as modern text: egoism, alienation, and suicide

I have started with Mr Golyadkin because he exemplifies many of Dostoevsky's most characteristic strategies, all of which are multi-layered and interconnected. Thematically, he takes an idea and pushes it to an extreme. In *The Double*, Dostoevsky brilliantly portrays a modern divided self who doubles before our eyes. In *Notes from Underground* (1864), he ingeniously places his critique of 'rational egoism', a theory of human nature promoted by 1860s radical critics, into the mouth of a real egoist. In *Crime and Punishment* (1866) and *Demons* (1871), he demonstrates how rationalist, materialist, utilitarian theories can lead to and be used to justify murder. In *The Brothers Karamazov* (1879–80), Dostoevsky ratchets up the religious dimension, asking how can there be morality without God.

Yet even when Dostoevsky shows how theory can drive action, he never loses sight of character psychology. Behind all motives and theories lurk the dangers of ego, such as narcissism, pride, and greed. Dostoevsky's greatest villains calculate: they are egoists who put themselves first and use others for their own advantage (like Luzhin, from *Crime and Punishment*). But many characters suffer from divided selves, especially Raskolnikov, whose name derives from the word for schism (*raskol*). Razumikhin (*Crime and Punishment*) diagnoses his friend Raskolnikov's self-division:

> 'I've known Rodion [Raskolnikov's first name] for a year and a half: sullen, gloomy, arrogant, and proud; recently (and maybe much earlier) touchy and hypochondriacal. Magnanimous and kind. He doesn't express his feelings and would rather commit a cruelty than express his heart with words. At times, however, he's not hypochondriacal at all, just inhumanly cold and unfeeling, exactly as though there were two opposing characters in him, changing places with one another.' (Pt III, ch. 2)

The best characters, like Prince Myshkin (*The Idiot*, 1868) and Alyosha Karamazov, acknowledge their doubleness. Myshkin confesses to the boxer Keller: 'Two ideas occurred together, that happens often. With me it's non-stop. I, by the way, think it's not good... for it is terribly difficult to fight with these double thoughts; I've experienced it' (Pt II, ch. 11). Alyosha, who is extremely chaste, confesses to his brother Dmitry that he, too, experiences the Karamazov sensuality (Bk III, ch. 4). Such statements underscore the universality of double thinking. Their manifestation in positive characters encourages reader identification with the phenomenon.

Dostoevsky's work as a whole abounds in character doubles, who serve as mirrors for other characters. In *Crime and Punishment*, many characters reflect some aspect of Raskolnikov. Razumikhin is an equally impoverished ex-university student, who chooses to work hard and help others rather than to quit tutoring and commit murder. Mikolka the painter confesses to Raskolnikov's crime, forcing Raskolnikov to confront his guilt. Svidrigailov and Raskolnikov both contemplate suicide on the same night, but only

Svidrigailov kills himself. The Prince Myshkin of Dostoevsky's notebooks for *The Idiot* splits into the saintly prince and the darkly passionate merchant's son Rogozhin in the novel. General Ivolgin plays fallen man to Nastasya Filippovna's fallen woman (*The Idiot*). Shatov and Kirillov reflect Stavrogin's contradictory (and discarded) ideological positions back to him in *Demons*. Most memorably, Ivan Karamazov generates a nightmare devil, who exposes him to himself: 'You are the embodiment of me myself, but only one side…of my thoughts and feelings, only the most nasty and stupid ones' (Bk XI, ch. 9). Each of these characters in their own way reflect another character back to themselves, encouraging readers to do the same.

Like so many other Dostoevskian characters, Mr Golyadkin experiences 'indescribable anguish', which derives from his identity crisis, particularly his separation from self and others. With each work he writes, Dostoevskian anguish becomes increasingly metaphysical. Later characters—like the underground man, Raskolnikov, the ridiculous man ('Dream of a Ridiculous Man', 1877), and Ivan Karamazov—not only feel alienated from self and others, but from God. In decrying the materialism he sees around him, the underground man pleads, 'Destroy my desires, wipe out my ideals, show me something better, and I will follow you' (Pt I, ch. 10). The ridiculous man is saved from suicide by a little girl who unsettles his conscience, effecting a dream vision that restores his faith in something greater than himself: 'How can I not believe: I saw the truth,—not that acquired by my mind, but saw, saw, and its *living image* will fill my soul forever' (Pt V). Ivan Karamazov's devil decries his job of negation and thrice voices the desire to be incarnated as a 250-pound merchant's wife who lights candles to God (Bk XI, ch. 9). The anguish of their identity crises becomes increasingly metaphysical. With Ivan's devil, the crisis takes a satirical turn: Ivan's devil desires to be his antithesis—a stout, religious housewife (Bk XI, ch. 9).

Throughout his 1870s *DW*, Dostoevsky links suicide to lack of belief in God, but in the 1840s and 1860s, he also ties suicide to self-assertion. In the 1840s/60s, Mr Golyadkin links his ambition and self-damaging behaviours to suicide—a social problem that haunts 1860s and 1870s Russia and Dostoevsky's oeuvre. After his servant Petrusha says that good people don't come 'in twos', Mr Golyadkin exclaims to himself: 'I'm a murderer [literally a soul-slayer, *dushegubets*], I'm, I'm a suicide, that's what I am!...there's still vanity [*ambitsiya*], say, my honour's suffering, say, you must save your honour! Suicide that I am!' (ch. 9). Mr Golyadkin's pronouns also reveal his self-division—'I'/'my' and 'you'/'yours'. Raskolnikov also links his ego to his crime, 'Was it the old crone I killed? I killed myself, not the old crone' (Pt V, ch. 4). The convicts who court life-threatening beatings (*Dead House*, 1861, Pt II, ch. 3), the consumptive Ippolit (*Idiot*), and the engineer Kirillov (*Demons*) all view suicide or suicidal behaviour as a way of asserting their individuality in a world over which they have no control (prison, impending death, loss of God). Svidrigailov and Stavrogin die by suicide because they find nothing more to live for. As Amy Ronner points out, Dostoevsky is a suicidologist, who explores many kinds of self-murder. Mr Golyadkin's splitting is just one of them.

Epistemic uncertainty and the fantastic

Throughout his work, Dostoevsky also explores the boundary between the real and the fantastic. He creates uncertainty about the existence of Mr Golyadkin's double. On the day after the double appears, for example, the narrator notes that no one, absolutely no one, could tell 'which one was the real (*nastoyashchii*) Golyadkin, and which was the counterfeit (*poddel'nyi*), who was the old and who the new, who was the original and who the copy' (ch. 6). He creates uncertainty about the existence of the letter Mr Golyadkin receives from Klara encouraging him to rescue her: he finds it in his pocket in the tavern (ch. 11), but it later disappears (ch. 13). Moreover, while Klara is its purported author, its language is Golyadkin's. When Svidrigailov first visits Raskolnikov (*Crime and Punishment*), the latter wonders whether Svidrigailov is a continuation of his dream (Pt IV, ch. 1). Prince Myshkin cannot determine whether the eyes he feels burning into him are real or not (*Idiot*; Pt III, ch. 10). And Ivan Karamazov's devil taunts Ivan for believing in his existence: 'I'm leading you alternately between belief and disbelief, and I have my own purpose in doing so. A new method, sir: when you've completely lost faith in me, then you'll immediately start convincing me to my face that I am not a dream but a reality' (Bk XI, ch. 9). Whether in gothic or comic mode, Dostoevsky uses epistemic uncertainty to hint at things we cannot grasp with rationality alone.

Dostoevsky and humour

Although Dostoevsky writes about serious psychological, social, and metaphysical issues, he does so with profound humour. In *The Double*, Dostoevsky uses irony, parody, hyperbole, and over-the-top gothic intensification, often all together. He deploys irony's double edge, both elevating and diminishing Mr Golyadkin by calling him 'our hero'. Mr Golyadkin meets his double on a gothically clichéd dark and stormy night. As he races up the staircase after his double, Mr Golyadkin's heart freezes, he is 'beside himself'. Entering his apartment, all Mr Golyadkin's 'premonitions' were realized, his breathing 'broke off', his head 'spun', he wanted to scream but could not, his hair stood on end, he sits down in horror: 'And there was reason for it. Mr Golyadkin absolutely recognized his night-time friend. His night-time friend was none other than he himself—Mr Golyadkin himself, a different Mr Golyadkin, but absolutely the same as he himself,—in a word, what is called his double in all respects' (ch. 5). This cliché-ridden, hyperbolic description conveys the finality as well as the horror of this realization. Horror and humour. Classic Dostoevsky.

Elsewhere in *The Double*, we witness the comic and terrifying proliferation of Mr Golyadkin's likenesses. Dostoevsky pulls out all the stops as his narrator claims that he would need to be a poet, at least as talented as Homer or Pushkin, to describe the magnificent celebration of Klara Olsufeevna's thoroughly mediocre bureaucratic name-day party (ch. 4). On a later gothic dark and stormy night, as Mr Golyadkin sits outside the Berendeevs' house, he blames Klara (who already has a fiancé), French novels, and her immoral upbringing (all clichés) for his elopement fantasy. As Mr Golyadkin and his double share secrets on their first night together, they comically touch on the metaphysical and agree that 'There's no one like God' (ch. 7). Word play abounds in the novella: Mr Golyadkin's night-time 'friend'/*priyatel'* is also his enemy/*nepriyatel'*; his 'friend'/*drug* is also other/*drugoi*; the 'stranger'/*neznakomets* is also his acquaintance, his familiar/*znakomets*: 'The thing is, that this stranger [*neznakomets*] now appeared to him somehow familiar [*znakomym*]' (ch. 5). In short, while Dostoevsky engages his readers affectively and thematically, he also delights us intellectually. Reading Dostoevsky is a full cognitive and affective experience.

Doubling and the human condition

Although Dostoevsky felt that his inability to find the right form for *The Double* spoiled his idea, he believed in its significance. His 11 April 1880 letter to Ekaterina Yonge may help to explain that his idea concerns the modern divided self:

> You write about your duality? But that's the most ordinary trait of human beings...That's why you are so dear to me, because this *doubleness* in you is exactly the same as in me, and it has been my whole life. It is a great torment, but at the same time a great pleasure. It is the strong consciousness, the necessity for self-accounting and the presence in your nature of the necessity of moral duty to yourself and to humanity. That's what this duality signifies.

In addition to considering duality an integral part of human nature—a part of consciousness, awareness of both self and other—Dostoevsky thus attributes a moral dimension to self-division. He opposes altruism (conscience, duty to others) to egoism (self-centredness, sense of superiority). In attributing a positive valence to altruism, Dostoevsky argues against the narcissism and self-importance of egoism. His lifelong, enormously influential exploration of the moral dimensions of human duality began with *The Double*.

Chapter 3
Freedom and polyphony:
Notes from Underground

Mikhail Bakhtin, the 20th-century critic, believed that meaning was acquired in dialogue, with every utterance anticipating or responding to another voice. As he rightly observed, Dostoevsky's imagination is deeply dialogic. His many and varied characters reveal themselves as much in words as in deeds. Dostoevsky's frequently unreliable narrators, like the narrator-chronicler in *Demons*, are often a single voice in a chorus of character voices forcing readers to engage in a fictional world that requires interpretation and judgement. But Dostoevsky also uses his dialogic imagination to reveal a character's monologism—as in *Notes from Underground*, whose unreliable first-person narrator champions free will while telling a life story that reveals his unfreedom, including his dependence on others for a sense of self. Similarly, Dostoevsky's most polyphonic novel, *The Brothers Karamazov*, not only provides a compendium of voices and genres, but also the strongest example of a fictional monologic voice—Ivan Karamazov's Grand Inquisitor (Book 5), a powerful authority figure who repudiates Christ's message of love and advocates unfreedom. Finally, Dostoevsky's dreamscapes are likewise monologic or polyphonic: conscious daydreams (like Raskolnikov's decision to kill the old pawnbroker) tend to be monologic, whereas unconscious dreams (like Raskolnikov's dream of the killing of the mare or the ridiculous man's dream of travelling to another planet and corrupting its inhabitants) tend to be polyphonic.

Paradox and dialogue

To demonstrate Dostoevsky's complex use of dialogue in addressing the concept of freedom, let us start with the narrator-hero of *Notes from Underground*. The underground man, whom critics sometimes identify as 'the paradoxicalist', embodies shame's paradox—its capacity to isolate yet connect. Though he has isolated himself, he reaches out to readers. Though he champions free will, he acts unfreely: since he lacks freedom, he desires what he doesn't have. By creating a disjuncture between the underground man's words and deeds, Dostoevsky reveals that which his hero would conceal. He fashions a first-person narrator whose overtly dialogic narrative strategies are actually monologic defences that both reveal his shame and limit his freedom. In doing so, Dostoevsky explores the psychological and metaphysical relationship between shame and unfreedom.

A drama of shame and guilt

The underground man's shame makes him universal. According to the biblical myth informing Dostoevsky's understanding, shame originates in the Fall. After transgressing in the Garden, Eve and Adam become self-conscious. Realizing their nakedness, they hide themselves. Expelled from the Garden, they lose their unselfconscious relationship to one another, their environment, and God. Dostoevsky explicitly locates his underground man in this fallen world. Like our mythical forebears, Dostoevsky's antihero has lost his sense of wholeness and belonging and thus experiences shame and self-consciousness. Just as Eve and Adam fabricate clothes that conceal their physical nakedness but reveal their transgression, so the underground man fabricates an egoistic philosophy that conceals the narcissistic, shame-based psychology that his autobiography reveals.

Dostoevsky links the underground man's metaphysics and his ethics through the narrative of his guilt and shame. As mentioned earlier, shame is broadly linked to human identity; guilt is more narrowly attributed to human action. Shame arises from feelings of exclusion, objectification, or negative self-assessment; guilt from transgression of personal, moral, social, or legal norms. Shame and guilt can be related, but need not be. For instance, the underground man's unattractive appearance makes him feel shame not guilt. When he passes his shame on to Liza by raping her, then paying her, however, he acts in a way that harms her and haunts him. He also compounds his original shame with the shame of knowing that he is the kind of person who has deliberately harmed another. In creating a character who hides his guilt behind a confession of shame that he aggressively generalizes to include his readers, Dostoevsky complicates his narrative.

Guilt often follows a sequence—transgression, repentance, expiation, and, in Christian scenarios, redemption. Shame has no fixed script. Nor can a single action heal feelings of shame. The underground man responds to shame by excluding, objectifying, and negatively assessing others; by struggling to be perceived as a worthy self-presenting agent; or by actively sharing his shame—contradictory responses that also characterize his writing project. He exposes himself partly to relieve his guilt and isolation, but he fails. To expiate his evil action, he must acknowledge its evil. Yet to do so, he must accept universal moral norms, which, as Dostoevsky shows, the underground man will not do. His egoism, as seen in his monologism, undermines his stated ethics. The underground man repeatedly chooses aggressive self-protection over the vulnerability of relation. When Liza offers herself to him freely, for example, he insults her by giving her money. Instead of appealing to our common experience of shame as grounds for bonding, he claims shame superiority: 'As far as I myself am concerned, I have merely taken to an extreme in my life what you have not dared to take even halfway' (Pt II, ch. 10).

Double-voicedness: author and hero in Part I

By granting the underground man radical individuality, autonomy, and freedom in making his own life choices, Dostoevsky creates a protagonist that existentialist thinkers will embrace as their forebear. By having his first-person narrator elaborate a philosophy that justifies inaction while arguing for free will, Dostoevsky reveals the flaws in his character's arguments. By creating a gap between author and character-narrator, Dostoevsky demonstrates that his narrator is emotionally stuck in an underground of his own making. Hell is not other people, but his own construct—as readers learn in Part II, when the underground man tells his story.

From the outset of *Notes*, Dostoevsky double-voices his character-narrator's words, that is, he exposes his narrator's psyche behind his back. Thus, the famous first lines of Part I—'I am a sick person...I am a spiteful/evil person. I am an unattractive person'—demonstrate his authorial control. For example, when the underground man announces that he is 'sick' and that his liver hurts, he encourages readers to regard his illness as physical, an explanation he subsequently repudiates. As Olga Meerson demonstrates, however, Dostoevsky the author uses this diagnosis to suggest metaphysical illness: the underground man alludes to Galen's theory of humours, but Dostoevsky alludes to the Old Testament Book of Lamentations. While his underground narrator remains resolutely earthbound, Dostoevsky suggests that he suffers from metaphysical desolation due to separation from God.

The underground man's second adjective, 'spiteful', reinforces the story's metaphysical dimension, for he uses the Russian word *zloi*, which also means 'evil'. The underground man encourages the psychological reading by constantly emphasizing his spitefulness. Dostoevsky, however, evokes the concepts of 'good' and 'evil', thereby suggesting a relationship between spite and evil. The sentence's central placement reveals Dostoevsky's authorial emphasis.

The third adjective, 'unattractive', reads as awkwardly in Russian as in English. The first two adjectives 'sick' and 'spiteful' are not only short and common, they rhyme—*bol'noi/zloi*. The underground man's third, multisyllabic, non-rhyming adjective—*neprivlekatel'nyi*—thus strikes a dissonant chord. Literally translated 'unattractive', the adjective can refer to physical appearance or moral qualities. Not surprisingly, the underground man focuses on his appearance, a major source of his shame-sensitivity, while Dostoevsky focuses on his moral condition. The underground man's first words dramatize his obsession with how others perceive him. His last adjective reveals that he frets more about his identity than his ethics—'I hated my face, for example, found it odious' (Pt II, ch. 1). The adjectival progression—sick, spiteful/evil, unattractive—also reflects the story's structure: the underground man aggressively exposes himself, yet, here as elsewhere, he places the most painful revelation last.

Aggressive confession: words and actions in Part II

The aggression of these opening sentences prepares readers, as much as anything can, for the hostility that follows. Most strikingly, the underground man aggressively assaults his readers with a narrative strategy that reflects his behaviour in the story: just as he aggressively passes his shame on to Liza, so he aggressively passes it on to his readers. In Part II, Dostoevsky has the underground man explain the dynamics of passed-on shame to Liza:

> You've come because I spoke *pitiful words* [*zhalkie slova*] to you then. So you went soft and wanted 'pitiful words' again. So know, know that I was laughing at you then. And I'm laughing now. Why are you trembling? Yes, I was laughing! I had been insulted earlier at dinner by the fellows who came ahead of me. I came there to thrash one of them, an officer. But I didn't succeed, I didn't find him. It was necessary to avenge my offence on someone, to take my own back, you turned up, and I poured out my spite on you and laughed. I had been humiliated, so I wanted to humiliate; I had been ground into a rag, so I too wanted to show power… (Pt II, ch. 9)

With these words, Dostoevsky reveals how passing on shame can lead to guilt but requires the humiliation of another. Humiliated by others, the underground man goes to a brothel where he assaults Liza sexually. When he wakes up and tries to have a conversation with her, he gets carried away by his own sentimentality. When she notes that he sounds as though he's speaking from a book, 'a wicked feeling' took hold of him. Failing to see that he has touched her emotionally, he proceeds to humiliate her verbally. Liza arrives at his lodging for their second meeting just as he is raging impotently at his servant Apollon. This time he assaults her verbally—because she has witnessed his humiliation in front of his servant—then sexually—because she has witnessed him break down and cry. When Liza leaves, the underground man turns on his readers. He switches from addressing his audience with the second-person plural 'you' to the first-person plural 'we': 'we've all become unaccustomed to life, we're all lame, each of us more or less' (Pt II, ch. 10).

The underground man's assaults on Liza and his readers explain his failure. Imprisoned by egoism and shackled by shame, he cannot envision true freedom. He defines free will negatively and thus fails to recognize its positive manifestation in Liza. The underground man adopts the form of confession for his *Notes*, but he cannot escape his bad conscience because, as Robert Belknap has noted, he does not repent. Confession can provide relief for both shame and guilt only if the one confessing gives his audience the authority either to accept him as he is (shame) or to forgive his transgression (guilt). The underground man refuses to relinquish authority because he fears loss of control. By repeatedly choosing egoism and isolation over relation and community, he fortifies his prison. Failure to repent cannot be overcome by confession alone.

Self and other

The underground man's repetition compulsion further limits his freedom. He not only assaults Liza twice following humiliation by others and twice following emotional exposures before her, he also forces himself on those who do not seek his company—first the officer on the sidewalk (with whom he has an imaginary duel), then his classmates (at a dinner to which he was not invited), then his servant (whom he refused to pay), and finally Liza. Dostoevsky uses this progression both to stress his antihero's ethical inertia and to characterize gender politics. The underground man cannot dominate his male interlocutors, so he channels his rage onto his female interlocutor.

His writing also repeats a pattern: the underground man feels so marginal, he creates dialogic situations to prove he exists. Thus, when he chooses to write his 'notes', he constructs readers with whom he acts out his patterns of behaviour. His sense of shame leads him to expose himself; exposure inevitably leads to more shame, which leads to flight—isolation, intellectualizing, fantasizing, or a combination. Fortified by his defences, he sallies forth aggressively, only to be defeated yet again. Repeat cycle.

These repetitions prepare us for his project's ultimate failure, for in his notes, the underground man turns on us, his imaginary interlocutors. He periodically exchanges his habitual first-person singular pronoun 'I' for the collective 'we', projecting his beliefs or habits onto his readers, as he does when speaking of Russian romantics—'We Russians' (Pt II, ch. 1)—or as he does in his final paragraph:

> Permit me, ladies and gentlemen, I am not justifying myself with that 'all of us'. As for what touches me personally, I have only in my life taken to an extreme that which you have not dared to take even halfway...We are even oppressed at being humans, humans with *our own* real bodies and blood; we are ashamed of it, we consider it a disgrace, and we keep trying to be some sort of fable-like universal beings.   (Pt II, ch. 10)

The argument of the paragraph (including the omitted parts) runs as follows: I am part of all of us (we). I do what you do, only I go further (I). We are all fallen creatures; we are all ashamed of ourselves; we are all seeking to be other than what we are (we). Inside his universalizing claim, the underground man grandiosely declares superiority. Instead of alleviating his shame by sharing it, he aggressively places himself first, isolating himself from the community he longs to join.

His writing project as explained in Part II thus resembles the toothache he discusses in Part I. The hypothetical toothache is an image of pain. Unlike Cleopatra's golden pins—an image that the underground man uses to represent pain inflicted by someone more powerful—or the slap in the face—which represents pain inflicted by a social equal—the toothache is a form of bodily pain. It thus resembles mortality, a source of shame that Dostoevsky's Ippolit, a young man dying of consumption, will rail against in *The Idiot*. Faced with this hypothetical evidence of his human condition, the underground man posits two responses: seeking help or suffering in silence. The first strategy he rejects early when he declares that he refuses to accept medical help 'out of spite' (Pt I, ch. 1). Though he later explains this decision in terms of free will, another dynamic actually obtains. To accept medical help requires acknowledgement of the doctor's superior knowledge or skill, and, as Belknap shows, the underground man refuses to acknowledge others' authority. He also rejects silent suffering. If he must suffer, he wants others to acknowledge his pain and suffer with him. By analogy, Dostoevsky reveals that the underground man's pleasure in writing derives from embellishing his pain and thus sharpening others' awareness of him. Faced with isolation and exclusion, he chooses self-exposure. Like his interlocutor Rousseau in *Confessions* (1782), the underground man forces others to acknowledge his presence, revels in his revelations of shame, and acts out a script—a concept developed by critic Sarah Young and applied to the later novel *The Idiot*—in which he is the primary actor.

Writing as an existential project

The underground man's defences thus expose the causes of his failure: while he addresses an audience, he wants to feel in control. Because he is socially inept, he feels most in control when alone. But when he is alone, there is no one to admire him—or even to acknowledge his existence. He writes in order to be. His writing becomes an existential project which takes the form of self-aggrandizement. He draws attention to himself to undo the pain of his insignificance. Exposing himself may be painful, but it proves he is alive. As he says in Part I: 'Well, even though the same result obtains with consciousness, that is, one will also do nothing, at least one can sometimes whip oneself, which livens it up somewhat' (Pt I, ch. 9). Even pain is better than inertia.

Throughout his *Notes*, the underground man claims moral superiority by declaring superiority for his self-consciousness. But such a claim rings hollow in the face of Liza's magnanimity. He argues for self-awareness; she demonstrates awareness of others. She offers him love. However, because she has witnessed his humiliation, he perceives her offer as a threat to his autonomy and thus his power to control his image, so he aggressively punishes her. His egoism blinds him, but not Dostoevsky's readers. We see that Liza embodies the elusive ideal the underground man cries out for at the end of Part I: 'Well, change, seduce me with something else, give me another ideal' (Pt I, ch. 10). Liza shows him something better—love and compassion, a way out of his prison house of shame.

Free will

The underground man's longest argument about free will comes in Part I, when he contends that his imaginary opponents' theories do not account for free will, even though it is man's 'most advantageous advantage'. Free will proves man is an independent agent who can choose to act against his own perceived or material advantage. Exerting free will in defiance of the laws of nature may be irrational, but it also proves his individual superiority. He may harm himself by refusing medical help, but he also asserts his autonomy by exercising choice. Throughout Part II, the underground man provides concrete examples of how he has harmed himself through exercising free will. He chooses to give up the prestigious civil service job he was offered in order to cut ties with his past. For seven long years he lives with Apollon, who torments him. He engages in a one-sided duel. He invites himself to the celebratory dinner for his former classmate Zverkov and behaves rudely.

In these cases, the underground man chiefly harms himself. But in both encounters with Liza, he inflicts deep suffering on another. When the underground man argues theoretically against the view that individuals always act in accordance with their perceived best interests and argues instead that humans do not always act rationally, he commands reader agreement. When he advocates ethical egoism, that is, a theory which holds individuals free to act upon their desires, he gives us pause. When he acts on his desire to harm rather than to help Liza, we are forced to re-evaluate his theory. By structuring the narrative this way, Dostoevsky reveals that the underground man's theory of free will is negative and reactive. He protests against his opponents, but he proposes no alternative. Since free will involves resisting desires as much as acting upon them, Dostoevsky demonstrates that his antihero reacts more than he acts. He may advocate free will, but he does not act freely—he fears others' responses, both imaginary and real. Here and elsewhere Dostoevsky addresses the issue of free will by focusing in on one key aspect—the character's unfreedom in the context of social relationships.

Dostoevsky continually underscores the disjuncture between the underground man's theory and his practice. While the underground man proclaims that free will manifests personality and individuality, he repeatedly exhibits lack of moral imagination. He longs for an identity but has no idea what he would choose to be (Pt I, ch. 6). He fantasizes but steals his plots from books (Pt II, ch. 2). He pines for the sacred but cannot comprehend it (Pt I, ch. 10). He senses something missing, but he cannot conceptualize it because it is outside him. His self-enclosure verges on solipsism. He cannot understand Liza, because she represents something truly other, an emotional intelligence not based on calculation. She thus haunts him.

In Part II, the underground man confesses that in order to live safely and vicariously he engages in reactive hero-fantasies derived from his reading:

> For example, I triumph over everyone; everyone, of course, is lying in the dust and is forced to voluntarily acknowledge all my perfections, and I forgive them all. I fall in love, being a famous poet and court chamberlain; I receive countless millions and donate them immediately to mankind, and then and there confess before all the world my disgraces, which, of course, are not mere disgraces, but contain an exceeding amount of 'the beautiful and the lofty', of something Manfredian. Everyone weeps and kisses

me (what blockheads they'd be otherwise), and I go barefoot and
hungry to preach new ideas and crush the retrograde under
Austerlitz.   (Pt II, ch. 2)

While others populate his fantasies, the underground man is the
sole actor. His fantasies, moreover, replicate his text's structure:
seemingly open to readers, his notes are actually closed. The
underground man's contemporaries and his readers are cast as the
conquered or the adulatory or both. His rootedness in scripted
hero fantasies renders him unfree.

Trapped in monologue

Dostoevsky the author and his underground narrator both
emphasize the latter's self-enclosure. The underground man
simply cannot envision a relationship based on mutuality. As he
confesses: 'with me to love meant to tyrannize and to excel
morally. For my whole life I have been unable even to imagine any
other kind of love.... Even in my underground dreams I did not
imagine love as anything but a struggle' (Pt II, ch. 10). His view of
love as a power struggle locks him into a dynamic that permits
only two outcomes—mastery or submission: 'I began it always
with hatred and ended it with moral subjugation, and afterwards
I never could imagine what to do with the subjugated object'
(Pt II, ch. 10). By choosing to see others as hated objects rather
than prospective equals, the underground man denies himself the
possibility both of meaningful relationships and of self-knowledge.
In creating the world in his own image without real dialogue, he
perpetuates his self-enclosure.

The underground man's failure to manage his self-image causes
him shame. His fear that he is not a qualified self-presenting
agent pervades the discourse of Part I and drives the action of
Part II. In the autobiographical part of his story, each incident he
relates follows a similar pattern—shame-exposure-exclusion-more
shame, etc. By witnessing this repetition, Dostoevsky's readers

see that to escape the underground means stepping out of this vicious cycle.

Liza represents a way out. Like the underground man, Liza is isolated, humiliated, and poor. She also erects stone wall defences. Yet when she sees the underground man's pain, she opens up to him as a fellow sufferer. Dostoevsky employs Liza not only as an alternative to the underground man, but as a model reader and interlocutor. At first she only hears the underground man assault her, but gradually she sees through his defences and empathizes with the suffering behind them: 'Liza, offended and crushed by me, understood much more than I had imagined. From all of it, she understood what a woman, if she loves sincerely, always understands above all, and that is: that I myself am unhappy' (Pt II, ch. 9). Like Liza, we are meant to see the misery behind the underground man's words. Liza escapes his monologizing script, because she reads the underground man with emotional intelligence and acts out of compassion. She challenges his solipsism by acting as an equal self-presenting agent. The underground man, however, sees her autonomy as a threat. His standard domination self-defence, cruelty and violence, fails.

He can boast success with the sabre-rattling petitioner in his office and declare victory with the sidewalk duel. He can pretend success when borrowing money from his supervisor for his evening out with friends. But he cannot repress the memory of Liza's compassion. Her generosity shames him. His shame-based cruelty (paying for her freely offered sex) haunts him. He does not harm the sabre-rattler, the officer, or his classmates. He harms Liza. AND he cannot save face—either before himself or his readers. So, just as he turns on Liza for witnessing his shame, he turns on us. He says to her:

> Have you really not even now guessed that I will never forgive you for having found me in this bathrobe when I was throwing

myself like a spiteful cur at Apollon...The saviour, the former
hero throwing himself like a mangy mongrel at his lackey, who
laughed at him. And for my tears just now, which I, like a shamed
woman, could not hold back in front of you, I will never forgive
you. And for that which I've just now confessed to you, I will also
never forgive *you*. (Pt II, ch. 9)

The same applies to his readers: he can never forgive us for
witnessing his shame, which he perceives as emasculating.

The underground man speaks loudly to readers because he
embodies shame's paradox. Perceiving the openness of relation as
a threat to his autonomy, he embraces isolation. Isolated, he longs
for connection. He reaches out to readers yet pushes us away.
His desire for audience approval conflicts with his fear of negative
response. Self-consciousness paralyses him. Dostoevsky
masterfully portrays this dialectic. In the person of the
underground man, Dostoevsky dramatizes shame's self-conscious
essence—its acute awareness of self and other. He creates a
narrator who constructs his text the way he protects his ego: his
shame defences and monologizing serve as narrative strategies
that allow Dostoevsky to reveal to his readers that which the
underground man would conceal from his readers. The
underground man writes aggressively. Every sentence is a
struggle: he intellectualizes yet emotes; he embraces yet rejects
isolation; he reveals yet represses his positive emotions; he
confesses self-loathing yet grandiosely declares his superiority; he
retreats into bookish fantasies which he tries to impose on others.
Yet the structure of his text—which is both his creation and
Dostoevsky's—exposes him. Brilliantly reversing the structure of
St Augustine's *Confessions*, which begins in autobiography and
ends in theology, Dostoevsky uses his underground man's
autobiography in Part II to discredit his philosophy in Part I.
By creating a character who boasts of his consciousness and
self-consciousness yet makes many unconscious, unself-aware
choices, a character who champions choice yet repeatedly chooses

to limit his own options, Dostoevsky demonstrates how his underground man's monologic shame defences, like denial or passing along his shame, make him unfree.

Ivan Karamazov's Grand Inquisitor

The greatest monologist in Dostoevsky's oeuvre is Ivan Karamazov's Grand Inquisitor. Unlike the underground man whose entire text is monologic, Ivan's Inquisitor is deeply embedded both in Dostoevsky's most polyphonic novel and in a conversation between Ivan and Alyosha about who has the right to forgive. Thus, despite the Inquisitor's multi-page monologue, in which he insists on correcting the unnamed Christ's errors, there is a dual response—Christ responds to the Inquisitor in Ivan's text and Alyosha responds to Ivan in Dostoevsky's text. The Inquisitor attacks the concept of freedom, arguing that while Christ gave humans free will and the opportunity to believe and love freely, humans are weak and prefer miracle, mystery, and authority. The Grand Inquisitor insists on taking the burden of freedom onto himself, theoretically releasing his subjects from it, but he also deprives them of the opportunity to exercise their free will. The Grand Inquisitor is Ivan's fictional creation—and Dostoevsky's greatest statement of his atheistic opponents' position—but the theoretical argument against freedom loses its impact when Alyosha asks how the story ends. The unnamed Christ of Ivan's story kisses the Grand Inquisitor on the lips—a wordless gesture of forgiveness that undoes his disquisition. The kiss says that there is nothing that cannot be forgiven, even the Inquisitor's apostasy. Alyosha then plagiarizes Christ's gesture of forgiveness and kisses Ivan. As fitting in a polyphonic setting, each kiss is received differently. Christ's kiss burns in the Grand Inquisitor's heart, and he releases his prisoner. Alyosha's kiss, by contrast, delights Ivan as it proves that his brother has listened attentively. Likewise, the kiss demonstrates that, like the underground man's Liza, Alyosha has understood the anguish behind the Grand Inquisitor's rant and his brother's story.

Dostoevsky uses the underground man's rantings and the Grand Inquisitor's disquisition to demonstrate the closed nature of monological theoretical systems, thereby expressing a lifelong preoccupation with the dangers of theory, such as alienation from real life. Liza's embrace, Christ's kiss, and Alyosha's kiss all break the monologic frame and offer their interlocutors a way out of their self-enclosure. All are gestures of love; all break down the other's defences. But most importantly, they are gestures of response—of dialogue that moves beyond language. Free will can only be exercised in an open field. Theorizing closes those fields, puts up barriers, excludes the words and gestures of others. With the stories of the underground man and the Grand Inquisitor, Dostoevsky shows that freedom can only be exercised in dialogue, and that not all dialogue is verbal—an embrace, a kiss are also dialogic acts, performed by agents who choose or are moved to respond positively to the pain they hear.

Freedom and dreams

Beyond his manipulations of dialogue and monologue on the narrative level and in character interactions, Dostoevsky also illustrates freedom and lack of freedom by contrasting unconscious dreams and daydreams, or conscious fantasies. In *The Brothers Karamazov*, all three brothers have a dream: Alyosha dreams that he and Zosima are present at the Wedding at Cana; Dmitry dreams of a burnt-out village and a baby crying from hunger; Ivan dreams that he has a dialogue with his devil. Each of these dreams reveals the unconscious choices facing the dreamer: Alyosha makes peace with Zosima's death when he intuits the unity of all in Christ; Dmitry accepts his responsibility for others; and Ivan remains unconscious—leaving readers to guess whether he will choose the devil's path of discord or Christ's path of unity. The ridiculous man's unconscious dream also reveals his freedom of choice. Having decided upon suicide, the ridiculous man falls asleep. In his dream, a messenger visits and takes him on a journey to a prelapsarian world whose inhabitants know no evil. During their interactions, the innocent inhabitants learn to lie, and the narrator of 'The Dream of the Ridiculous Man' blames himself for corrupting them. Yet when he awakens, the ridiculous man feels with every fibre of his being that he has seen the truth—'Because I have seen the truth, I have seen and know that people can be beautiful and happy without losing the ability to live on earth. I do not wish and cannot believe that evil is the normal state of humankind' (Pt V). In short, the ridiculous man's unconscious dream converts him to a love of life and humankind.

While the unconscious dreams in *The Brothers Karamazov* and 'Dream of a Ridiculous Man' reveal the workings of the dreamers' psyches, in *Crime and Punishment*, Dostoevsky deliberately contrasts unconscious and conscious dreams in order to illustrate the difference between the freedom of the unconscious and the strictures of theory. We need only remember that Raskolnikov's unconscious dream of Mikolka killing the old mare temporarily releases him from 'this cursed daydream of mine', that is, his to kill the old pawnbroker. In this case as well, consciousness offers only one path—murder—while unconsciousness offers multiple interpretations and thus multiple choices. In his dream, Raskolnikov identifies with his younger self, with the old mare, and with Mikolka, the mare's murderer. Raskolnikov's unconscious dream thus puts him in touch with his moral emotions and offers him a way out of the straitjacket of his daydream of murder.

In all these cases, Dostoevsky ties true freedom and free will to dialogue—whether it be internal or external. Dostoevsky's powerful monologists, the underground man and the Grand Inquisitor, warn readers about people who remain tied to their theory. Monologic constructs create prisons with no way out. Dialogue offers choice and the freedom to exercise it.

Chapter 4
Space, social justice, and scandal: *Crime and Punishment*

Like Dickens and Balzac, Dostoevsky is a poet of the city. His city is Petersburg, whose simultaneously grand and gritty reality Dostoevsky knew intimately as trained engineer, voracious reader, and citizen. This broad background gave Dostoevsky a unique perspective on the city's contrastive topography and literary complexity, prompting him to develop the metaphorical dimension of realistic spaces—urban and non-urban, public and private. This chapter highlights spaces, both public and private, as the settings for social justice and scandal scenes. Moreover, just as *Dead House* and *The Double* provided a focus for my first two chapters, this chapter will mostly focus on *Crime and Punishment* and Petersburg. Then it will shift focus to scandal scenes, demonstrating that scandal can occur anywhere—Petersburg and Pavlovsk in *The Idiot*, an unnamed provincial town in *Demons*, a provincial town named once (Skotoprigonevsk) in *The Brothers Karamazov*.

Petersburg/*Crime and Punishment*

Dostoevsky's most famous Petersburg texts are *The Double*, *Notes from Underground*, and *Crime and Punishment*. Like all of Dostoevsky's mature work, *Crime and Punishment* operates on multiple levels—realistic, thematic, metaliterary, and metaphysical—often simultaneously. Petersburg, for example, is a real city built as Russia's window on the West by Peter the Great, who employed European architects as designers. Its founding is powerfully portrayed in Pushkin's narrative poem *The Bronze Horseman* as the triumph of Peter's vision: order over chaos, civilization over nature, granite river banks over unruly river. Yet Pushkin's poem also represents the costs of maintaining this created order: the Neva periodically overflows its granite banks, and citizens periodically revolt against imperial repression. Petersburg is thus a real city conceived as an imperial idea that is represented in literature as a creation myth, in other words, a struggle between chaos and the forces of order. In Dostoevsky's novel these levels of meaning open out onto broader themes of social inequity and metaphysics.

The social geography of Petersburg

On the realistic level, the major action of *Crime and Punishment* occurs in the poorer, crowded district around the Ekaterininsky Canal, also known as the Kanavka, or 'ditch', one of the four waterways at the mouth of the Neva built or enlarged to drain the marshes. The Moika, which was closest to the Neva, the Admiralty, and the Winter Palace, was flanked by government buildings and aristocratic palaces. Next came the meandering Ekaterininsky Canal, the poorer, more crowded area that was Dostoevsky territory. The river Fontanka was home to bureaucrats—the higher-ranked on the lower floors, the lower-ranked on the higher floors. This vertical hierarchy obtained for all rental buildings as well: the poorest Petersburgers packed into either the highest floors or the flood-prone basements. Furthest from the centre, the Obvodny Canal ran near Semyonovsky Square, the military parade ground where Dostoevsky's mock execution was staged.

These waterways were intersected by three grand boulevards radiating out from the Admiralty building—Nevsky Prospekt, Gorokhovaya Street, and Voznesensky Prospekt—all of which led to railway stations by the time of Dostoevsky's death. Across the river lay Vasiliyevsky Island, home to the university, beyond which lay smaller islands, home to parks and vacation houses. After his dream of the mare, in which the young protagonist Raskolnikov witnesses a peasant beat his aged horse to death, Raskolnikov wakes under a bush on Petrovsky Island. This open space represents a release from the crowding of the mainland and prefigures the open space of Siberia, where Raskolnikov will experience his spiritual transformation.

The waterways were also used to transport heavy goods—such as the hay sold in Haymarket Square, a central market featured in the novel. The drunkard Marmeladov, for instance, spends a night on a hay barge after his drinking spree. The pawnbroker's half-sister Lizaveta trades in used clothing in the Haymarket, where Raskolnikov overhears her making plans to be away from her stepsister's apartment the following evening. Seedy taverns, brothels, and flophouses like Vyazemsky's, where Dunya's suitor Svidrigailov claims to have spent the night in his younger days, surrounded the Haymarket. It is not surprising then that Raskolnikov meets and gives money to the prostitute Duklida on one of its side streets or that he finds Marmeladov in a seedy tavern nearby. Moreover, before surrendering himself to the police, Raskolnikov kneels down and kisses the earth amidst the Haymarket's bustle.

The novel's characters live in rental buildings, which were common in Petersburg. For example, Raskolnikov inhabits an attic room, a cheap lodging that symbolically signals his alienation from the life around him. The impoverished Marmeladovs live in a hallway, with only a curtain to protect their privacy. Sonya is so poor that she rents a room from a destitute family that need to sublet part of their living space. Dunya's fiancé Luzhin chooses to stay with Lebezyatnikov to save money. He also rents a low-budget room in a disreputable building for Dunya and her mother to economize on expenses while he renovates an apartment for his marriage. Raskolnikov's friend Razumikhin initially lives on

Vasiliyevsky Island near the university but moves to a rental building on the mainland not far from Raskolnikov.

Ideology and the theme of resurrection

On the thematic level, Dostoevsky's novel highlights the power of ideas. In the letter pitching his novel to Mikhail Katkov, the conservative editor of the successful monthly journal *Russian Herald*, Dostoevsky outlines a plot focused on a young university dropout who commits murder after becoming obsessed by 'certain strange "unfinished" ideas floating in the air' (10–15 September 1865). In 1860s Russia, these Western-derived ideas—atheism, materialism, utilitarianism, feminism, scientism—amalgamated into an ideology called 'nihilism'. While Dostoevsky parodies some of these ideas through the figure of Lebezyatnikov, he also portrays the deadly consequences of embracing a rationality-based ideology by depicting the character and fate of Raskolnikov.

Dostoevsky also links the themes of social justice and resurrection by referencing the two Lazaruses from the Gospels of Luke and John. In Luke, a rich man refuses to give even the crumbs from his table to the beggar Lazarus. When they die, Lazarus is taken up to heaven and the rich man is cast into hell, where Abraham refuses to have Lazarus deliver a drop of water for the rich man to drink, thereby reversing their positions both physically and spiritually (Luke 16: 19–31). This Lazarus became the subject of a spiritual song and 'to sing Lazarus' became a saying for telling a tale of woes. Significantly, Raskolnikov thinks of this song (Pt III, ch. 4) just before his first meeting with Porfiry Petrovich, the judicial investigator (Pt III, ch. 5). Towards the end of that meeting, Porfiry asks Raskolnikov if he believes in the literal raising of Lazarus from the grave (John 11). Dostoevsky connects these two by the name Lazarus but also by adding that the rich man from the Gospel of Luke was dressed 'in porfiry', that is, in rich purple cloth. Dostoevsky also connects the realistic and the religious by using the iconography of John's Lazarus rising from the dead throughout the text, including the scene when Raskolnikov buries the money and goods stolen from the pawnbroker under a large rock.

Petersburg literature

On the metaliterary level, Dostoevsky draws on Petersburg's rich literary tradition. As the novel opens, for example, Raskolnikov leaves his room on S- Lane (Stolyarni pereulok) and heads towards K- bridge (Kokushkin most), home both to Lermontov's hero Lugin ('Shtoss') and to one of the two canine correspondents in Gogol's 'Diary of a Madman'. Dostoevsky also extends the duality embedded in Petersburg texts by inscribing Raskolnikov's inner division into the cityscape. On his way to the pawnbroker's, for example, Raskolnikov avoids the shortest route, which would take him past the Voznesensky Church (a sacred space), and walks past the Yusupov Gardens (a secular space) instead. In this way, Raskolnikov symbolically avoids salvation while courting damnation. Yet the novel is not always so clear: several buildings—the Crystal Palace tavern, Razumikhin's building, and the district police station—have ambiguous locations, each with its own symbolic possibilities. For example, the police station could be either in the Saviour district or the Kazan district or, in Dostoevsky's world, both. Furthermore, by making it unclear whether Raskolnikov crosses the Bankovsky (Bank) Bridge to the left or the Voznesensky (Ascension) Bridge to the right as he leaves the Crystal Palace (named for the site of the 1851 Great Exhibition in London, symbol of modernity, and a central image of Dostoevsky's critique of Western rationalism), Dostoevsky keeps readers wondering whether Raskolnikov will choose the material or the spiritual path.

On the metaphysical level, the novel stages a battle for Raskolnikov's soul. After Raskolnikov kills the pawnbroker and her half-sister Lizaveta, he is spiritually dead. At the novel's centre (Pt IV, ch. 4), he visits Sonya Marmeladova and demands that she read him the story of Lazarus (Gospel of John 11). Sonya is a real prostitute, who is sustained by her faith in God, but her name is also the diminutive for Sophia, who serves as an intermediary between God and humans. Her name, which is used by Eastern Orthodox Christian believers to indicate Divine Wisdom, keeps the religious theme alive throughout the novel. The novel thus realistically, thematically, metaliterarily, and metaphysically poses the question of Raskolnikov's potential resurrection. In Part VI, Raskolnikov faces the choice of Sonya (confession) or Svidrigailov (escape/suicide). Before confessing, Raskolnikov bows down and kisses his mother Pulcheria and then stops in the Haymarket to bow down and kiss the earth (Mother Russia). Bowing down is an act of humility, recognition of something higher than oneself. Raskolnikov's three bows—to his mother and the earth in Part VI and to Sonya in the Epilogue—represent his turn away from self-isolation and alienation and his return to family, community, and God.

'Nowhere to go'

From his very first published work, *Poor Folk*, Dostoevsky's investigation of the problem of freedom leads him to trap his characters in confined spaces. He is also a master of setting important scenes in places—like shabby eating houses or drawing rooms—where the private and the public converge. In *Crime and Punishment*, Dostoevsky uses one such shabby eating house to emphasize the novel's social justice themes, which can be summarized by Marmeladov's phrase 'nowhere to go'. Returning from a test run to the pawnbroker's, Raskolnikov stops in a tavern, which served 'chopped pickles, dry black bread, and fish cut into pieces, all quite evil-smelling. It was so stuffy that it was almost impossible to sit there, and everything was so saturated with the smell of wine that it seemed one could get drunk in five minutes from the air alone' (Pt I, ch. 2). In this vividly described space, with other customers mocking him, a drunken Marmeladov holds forth, grandiloquently telling his story. He garners the reader's sympathy for himself and his family when he explains why he married Katerina Ivanovna:

> 'I could not look at such suffering. You may judge thereby what degree her calamities had reached, if she, well-educated, well-bred, from a well-known family, agreed to marry me! But she did!…For she had nowhere to go. Do you understand, do you understand, my dear sir, what it means when there is indeed nowhere else to go?'   (Pt I, ch. 2)

Marmeladov's iterated phrase 'nowhere to go' encapsulates the novel's emerging social justice themes—poverty, inequality, women's limited economic options—themes that will resonate not only in the Raskolnikov family story (Pt I, ch. 3) but throughout the novel.

Marmeladov's garrulous speech allows Dostoevsky to identify a systemic problem: the largely family-based Russian economy offered no social safety net for the poor. The phrase 'nowhere to go' highlights the desperation caused by poverty and underscores the era's gender dynamics: most women were almost entirely dependent on their families for support. Since the market for women's labour was exceedingly limited, if their family renounced them, or if the male breadwinner lost his job or died, women and their children had nowhere to go—but onto the streets. This is what Katerina Ivanovna asks Sonya, her stepdaughter, to do.

Marmeladov's speech provides gritty specifics about the social justice issues that haunt the text. He lost his job in the provinces due to a 'change of staff', indicating he was probably replaced because of nepotism. (It was common for those in power to replace staff to benefit their own family or to gain favour with their own superiors—whether or not there was a legitimate excuse, like drinking.) He brought his family to Petersburg, where he found and lost another job, this time due to his drinking. The shabby tavern thus represents another social problem—excessive drinking—that is both the cause and effect of the Marmeladovs' current poverty. Sonya's earlier attempts to support her family by working as a seamstress failed when a state councillor (a high-ranking, well-paid civil servant) refused to pay for the six shirts she had made him. This small loss of income broke the family economy, resulting in three days of near-starvation. Katerina Ivanovna then nagged Sonya into prostitution, accepted 30 silver roubles for this betrayal, and wept with her. Marmeladov responded to his daughter's fall by begging for another chance from his boss, working for a month, but then stealing the money remaining from his salary for a drinking spree. The story is Marmeladov's; the details are Dostoevsky's. Katerina Ivanovna's betrayal of Sonya for 30 pieces of silver adds a biblical layer to Dostoevsky's realist text about poverty and desperation. It also provides a cautionary tale regarding women's role in oppression, whether through money-lending or the grooming of daughters to satisfy male power.

Whatever sympathy Marmeladov's self-accusing rhetoric might have generated for him may well dissipate when Raskolnikov brings the drunken Marmeladov home and readers see the extent of the family's destitution. The Marmeladovs do not even have a room of their own—they live in the walk-through entry hall of a rental apartment. As other lodgers come and go, Katerina Ivanovna, who is dying of consumption, must endure waves of smoke. There the stick-thin, ill-clothed, uneducated Marmeladov children sleep behind a flimsy curtain; the entire family shares a single green shawl for warmth. The family is then evicted following a fabricated scandal in their living space. A despairing, half-mad Katerina Ivanovna takes her children to the streets—deliberately exposing their poverty and creating a public scandal. The phrase 'nowhere to go', introduced near the beginning of Part I, is thus literalized by the end of Part V. Moreover, both the Marmeladov living space and its loss underscore the family's marginality and that of countless other impoverished residents of Petersburg. Each item at the pawnbroker's could tell a similar tale of desperation.

St Petersburg vices: prostitution, drunkenness, usury

In the 1860s, prostitution was legal in Russia. Prostitutes were required to register with the police or medical authorities in their city. They carried an official document, the 'yellow ticket' (see Figure 6) which replaced their passport, and were subject to regular medical examinations to check for venereal disease. Like many other writers of the time, Dostoevsky was profoundly troubled by the problem of prostitution and 'the fallen woman' and addressed it in many of his works, most memorably *Notes from Underground* and *Crime and Punishment*.

The problem of alcoholism received a great deal of attention in Russia during the 1860s. Attempts to grapple with its social costs through regulation and policy were complicated by the fact that the sale of alcohol brought in significant revenue through excise taxes. The Marmeladov subplot of *Crime and Punishment*, and the novel's original working title, 'The Drunkards', reflects Dostoevsky's concern for this problem.

Moneylending was widespread in Dostoevsky's world. Until 1865, charging higher than 6 per cent interest was called usury (*likhva*), a criminal violation, but was widely practised secretly. The laws were relaxed in 1865. Aliona Ivanovna, the pawnbroker (and murder victim) in *Crime and Punishment*, sets a 10 per cent monthly interest rate—an annual rate of 120 per cent—reflecting a new trend in St Petersburg. Dostoevsky availed himself of the services of pawnbrokers during this period, and his depiction of the practice in his novel reflects his own personal experience.

Box credit: Carol Apollonio

6. A 'yellow ticket' issued to a Nizhny Novgorod prostitute in 1904.

As *Crime and Punishment* demonstrates, poverty makes families and individuals vulnerable in myriad ways. Hunger, illness, and homelessness threaten. Pawnbrokers and procuresses abound. When Raskolnikov reads his mother's letter (Pt I, ch. 3), Dostoevsky establishes links between the Marmeladovs and the Raskolnikovs—irresponsible men not supporting their families, mothers willing to sacrifice daughters, daughters sacrificing themselves for their families. Sonya Marmeladov is forced into prostitution. Raskolnikov's sister Dunya agrees to an unequal marriage that both her brother and her pursuer Svidrigailov consider the equivalent of selling herself. Raskolnikov protects a potential rape victim from the predatory male stalking her. He gives money to a prostitute on the street. Svidrigailov is haunted by the image of a young suicide whom he probably raped (Pt IV, ch. 2). Dostoevsky emphasizes the young girl's vulnerability by making her the deaf-mute niece of his landlady, Mme Resslich, a procuress who also arranges a young bride for him. Although 'nowhere to go' can end in suicide, as in the case of Mme Resslich's niece, Dostoevsky offers some ways out. Svidrigailov's deceased wife saves Dunya from Luzhin's clutches twice: first by leaving Dunya 3,000 roubles in her will, then by providing the pistol Dunya uses to ward off Svidrigailov's unwelcome advances. Furthermore, Sonya transcends her economic hardships through her faith in God, a faith that she offers to share with Raskolnikov at Epilogue's end.

'Nowhere to go' has another dimension—imperial Petersburg as the administrative capital is a place of ambition and of last resort. People come to the capital city to further their careers (Luzhin) and to petition the courts. A major's widow from the provinces living with her daughter in the same rented lodgings as the Marmeladovs, for instance, has come to Petersburg to petition for a pension (Pt V, ch. 2). Svidrigailov tells Raskolnikov of meeting and helping another mother–daughter pair of petitioners, recently arrived from the provinces, in a dance hall that they had mistaken for a dance studio (Pt VI, ch. 4). The idea of Petersburg as a place of last resort is not limited to *Crime and Punishment*. In *The Idiot*, for example, the consumptive Ippolit tells the story of a doctor who had come to Petersburg to petition for a new position (Pt III, ch. 6); a similar dynamic drives the plot of the 1861 novel *The Insulted and Injured*. Whereas Svidrigailov and Ippolit help the mother–daughter pair and the doctor, most petitioners do not meet a benefactor, and if their petitions are ignored or rejected, there is no further appeal—except to God. While faith in God can save one's soul, it does not necessarily protect from the perils of poverty. Many malnourished babes die in Dostoevsky's work.

In addition to its socio-political dimension, 'nowhere to go' has an existential dimension. The 20th-century literary theorist Mikhail Bakhtin hails Dostoevsky as a poet of the threshold—both figuratively—'Dostoevsky always represents a person *on the threshold* of a final decision, at a moment of *crisis*'—and literally—'The threshold, the foyer, the corridor, the landing, the stairway…and beyond these the city: squares, streets, facades, taverns, dens, bridges, gutters. This is the space of the novel [*Crime and Punishment*].' The pervasive sense of threshold gives Dostoevsky's work a sense of urgency. People in crisis feel out of place—they either do not fit into the existing hierarchies or they struggle with their assigned place. In Dostoevsky's work, crisis often leads to scandal—moments when the private explodes into public view. Unsurprisingly, scandal scenes abound in Dostoevsky's work.

Shame, public space, and scandal

Dostoevsky uses shame dynamics to implicate readers in the ethical action of his texts. Shame relates broadly to human identity and entails a global devaluation of self—feelings of inferiority, inadequacy, defectiveness, exclusion. Shame is usually experienced passively—often as a result of being objectified—which accounts for much of the pain it evokes. Shame's unexpectedness in particular allows Dostoevsky to unleash the affective and cognitive synergy of three properties of the shame experience—disruption, disorientation, and self-consciousness. Shame precipitates scandals, often 'suddenly' (*vdrug*), and scandals expose both personal shame and social ills. Dostoevsky's novels abound in theatrical scandal scenes in which private dramas become public. In *Crime and Punishment*, he exploits the private/public nature of the Marmeladovs' hallway-room to stage two private/public spectacles. The first is Marmeladov's death scene. When a drunken Marmeladov is brought home after being run over by a carriage, 'almost all of Mrs Lippewechsel's tenants came pouring from the inner rooms, crowding in the doorway at first, but then flooding into the room itself' (Pt II, ch. 7). Even though Katerina Ivanovna scolds them away, Marmeladov's death becomes a public spectacle. The second scandal ends with the Marmeladovs' eviction. At Katerina Ivanovna's tragicomic funeral meal for Marmeladov, Luzhin accuses Sonya of stealing money from him. Lebezyatnikov and Raskolnikov ultimately expose Luzhin for framing her, but the public accusation underscores poor women's vulnerability to the depredations of wealthier men. Once the Marmeladovs are evicted, Katerina Ivanovna brings the scandal of her family's poverty to the streets of Petersburg, where, like her husband, she falls, never to rise from her deathbed.

Scandal in the provinces

Dostoevsky figures the dynamics of shame not only in the iconic space of Petersburg, but in the provinces, which he treats as microcosms of the capital city. Many scandal scenes expose socio-economic inequities, for example, in multiple scenes in *The Idiot*, set both in Petersburg and in Pavlovsk. Although General Totsky in *The Idiot* abuses his ward Nastasya Filippovna, she is treated as a scandalmonger for exposing rather than accepting the double standard. By drawing parallels between Nastasya Filippovna as a fallen woman and the alcoholic General Ivolgin as a fallen general, Dostoevsky underscores gender politics and inequities. Though both Nastasya Filippovna and General Ivolgin experience shame and social exclusion, their lives and deaths differ radically. Ivolgin once had a place in society and the military, and he dies in the bosom of his family. By contrast, Nastasya Filippovna was orphaned, isolated, and abused while an adolescent, so she never belonged to the community that excludes her. Instead of accepting her non-place, Nastasya Filippovna shares her shame by shaming others.

In *Demons*, Dostoevsky stages a scandal in the drawing room, the private/public space where the noblewoman Varvara Stavrogina invites Marya Lebyadkina, a feeble-minded crippled person, and her socially unacceptable brother, the pretender Captain Lebyadkin. She asks her only son and heir Nikolai to explain his relation to Marya (whom he married on a whim). Varvara does not receive an answer, but the event itself is a scandal—the crossing of social boundaries. The novel's larger scandal comes at a much publicized and anticipated fundraiser for local governesses that gets infiltrated by forces of chaos. The local governesses are forgotten as the rabble demand food and drink. Social justice and scandal are conjoined in the person of Fedka the Convict, a serf lost at cards by Stepan Verkhovensky, the novel's resident intellectual and tutor to the younger generation. As a result of his sudden impoverishment, Fedka becomes a murderer and arsonist for hire: he murders the Lebyadkins and sets fire to their lodgings. In contrast to *Demons*, *The Adolescent* might be said to be a novel about avoiding scandal—all the major characters in the novel do everything they can to avoid scandal and keep the social structure intact. In the meantime, readers learn of all sorts of injustices—illegitimate children, unacknowledged marriages, illicit liaisons, blackmail.

As for *The Brothers Karamazov*, one of its earliest scenes is the scandal Fyodor Karamazov creates in the local monastery, another private/public space, where the Karamazov family has assembled to ask the Elder Zosima to mediate a family dispute. Fyodor's subsequent murder is not only presented as a local scandal, but becomes a national spectacle when the case goes to trial. Fittingly, Dostoevsky exposes the crux, making the murder of Fyodor Pavlovich not only a parricide, but because of his patronymic, a tsaricide, and, in keeping with the novel's metaphysical thematics, a deicide. Although his son Dmitry is accused and found guilty, Fyodor Pavlovich is actually murdered by his presumed illegitimate son Pavel Fyodorovich Smerdyakov, who imbibes Ivan Karamazov's credo that if God does not exist, all is permitted. Smerdyakov's illegitimacy means that he is out of place, unacknowledged. The scandal of his illegitimacy and the resentment it fosters make Smerdyakov, whose name means 'stinker' but also 'serf', a symbolic tsaricide—a subject who rises up against the legitimate tsar. It thus strikes a bell for Russian contemporaries who were aware that Paul I was probably killed by his subjects with the knowledge of his son Alexander II. Dostoevsky thus weaves Russian history into his fiction. By setting a lot of his work in the provinces, Dostoevsky did what many of his contemporaries did—he treated the provinces as microcosms of Russia which have many of the same problems as the capital city. In this way, he expanded the scope of the novel's action.

Universalizing the Petersburg text

This chapter began with Dostoevsky as a poet of the city and an analysis of his Petersburg text, *Crime and Punishment*, which, like all of Dostoevsky's mature work, operates on numerous levels simultaneously. This analysis demonstrates the way in which crisis figures into Dostoevsky's artistic perspective as well as the way in which crisis often leads to scandal—those moments when the private sphere is suddenly exposed to public view. Along with that ruptured partition between public and private is Dostoevsky's deployment of shame dynamics to implicate readers in the ethical actions of the texts. Such devices are not just present in *Crime and Punishment*, but also in *The Idiot*, *Demons*, *The Adolescent*, and *The Brothers Karamazov*. This urge to universalize creates a larger geography of the city through exploration of scandal in the provinces. It is ironic, however, that this poet of the city, who developed the metaphorical dimension of realist spaces—urban and non-urban, public and private—honed his artistry, absorbed others' stories, and cultivated his artistic vision during his four years of confinement and exile in Siberia. In his autobiographical novel, *Notes from the Dead House*, Dostoevsky created a fictitious narrator, Aleksandr Petrovich Goryanchikov, who shares his traumatic ordeal within the confines of Omsk Fortress. Although it is neither urban nor non-urban, that microcosm of convicts in Siberia offers a taste of both confinement and openness that prepares for the epilogue of *Crime and Punishment*, where the prisoner Raskolnikov looks across the river at a biblical landscape whose openness frames his spiritual change.

Chapter 5
Aesthetics and ethics:
The Idiot and *Demons*

Readers are drawn to Dostoevsky's writings for many reasons—their psychological depth, cultural insight, and perspectives on Russian social and political history, not to mention their riveting storytelling power and entertainment value. At their deepest level, Dostoevsky's works grapple with the big unanswerable questions of philosophy, focusing as they do on the relation between aesthetics and ethics. This was a natural pairing for two reasons. First, Dostoevsky had a classical view of beauty, ranking it as a metaphysical value along with the good: 'In the ancient Greek conception of *kalon*, the good, true, and beautiful work as an integral whole in their erotic pull.' Or, in Dostoevsky's words, 'Only that which coincides with your feeling of beauty and with the ideal in which you incarnate it is *moral*' (Notebooks for 1881 *DW*). Second, Dostoevsky was raised in the Russian Orthodox tradition, whose emphasis on beauty can be seen in its liturgy and iconography, both of which emphasize Christ's resurrection rather than his crucifixion. It is this pairing of ethics and aesthetics that lends special power to Dostoevsky's treatment of visual imagery and ekphrasis in his fiction.

The critic Robert Jackson identifies the two poles of Dostoevsky's aesthetics as *obraz*, form, and *bezobrazie*, or formlessness. In Dostoevsky's novels we are privy not only to characters' interactions but to their internal struggles to do what is right rather than what is easier, more satisfying, or more advantageous. In many cases, his characters are torn between God-given form and demonic formlessness. As Dostoevsky wrote in an article on devils, their kingdom is discord and their guiding motto is 'divide and conquer' (*DW* January 1876, ch. 3.2). He warns readers that those who idolize materialism are prime targets for demonic temptations and that those who deny devils' existence persecute believers, causing belief in devils to spread like a wildfire (*DW* January 1876, ch. 3.2).

The beautiful and the good

Dostoevsky's novel *The Idiot* powerfully dramatizes the fraught relationship between the beautiful and the good. The novel's main action is a love triangle that pivots around three main characters—Prince Myshkin, Parfen Rogozhin, and Nastasya Filippovna Barashkova. Nastasya Filippovna is a beautiful young woman whose guardian, Afanasy Totsky, abused her when she was younger and now wants to cast her off. As the novel begins, the narrator makes it clear that Nastasya Filippovna hates not only Totsky, but herself. The question posed throughout Part I is what will she do? Will she follow Totsky's script and marry Ganya Ivolgin, thereby freeing Totsky to marry someone else? Or will she act as Totsky fears and respond with resentment, anger, hatred, and the desire for revenge? In short, will this beautiful woman act from the goodness of her heart or react to the wrongs done her? Will her actions conform to her exterior beauty or not? Will the result be form or formlessness? Visual images convey the novel's aesthetic and ethical drama: a reproduction of Hans Holbein the Younger's grimly realistic painting of the dead Christ in the tomb hangs at the centre of Rogozhin's house and haunts the beautiful Nastasya Filippovna's plot.

Nastasya Filippovna's future depends on her ability to overcome her self-hatred. Before he meets her, Prince Myshkin looks at

Nastasya Filippovna's portrait and perspicuously observes: 'It's a proud face, terribly proud, but here's what I don't know, is it kind? Ah, if only it is kind! Everything would be saved!' (Pt I, ch. 3). In a typical Dostoevskian move, our author plays with a word's dual meaning to suggest the novel's metaphysical dimension: the Russian word for 'kind' (*dobro*) also denotes the moral quality 'good'. In a sense, the entire novel's outcome, as well as Nastasya Filippovna's fate, depends not only on whether or not she is kind/good, but also on whether she can accept and act from that part of herself. At her name-day party later that day, Nastasya Filippovna declares that for the past five years she has lost herself in 'spite' towards Totsky even while asking herself if he's worth such 'malice'. The words she uses for 'spite' (*zloba*) and 'malice' (*zlost'*) both derive from the same root as 'evil' (*zlo*), further emphasizing the metaphysical dimension of Dostoevsky's social drama. Dostoevsky keeps the concepts of good (*dobro*) and evil (*zlo*) alive throughout *The Idiot* by deploying words with those root meanings. Thus, while highlighting Nastasya Filippovna's beauty and the iconicity of her portrait, Dostoevsky also reminds readers of the metaphysical war within her that will determine how morally good her beauty will turn out to be.

Prince Myshkin's observation penetrates to the heart of the matter: will Nastasya Filippovna's past suffering help or hurt her? Will she act from the goodness of her heart, that is, morally, or will she turn away from the good and act perversely? Will she accept her changed social status, or will she punish herself for what was done to her? Throughout the novel, Nastasya must constantly decide between accepting offers of marriage from the novel's two other major characters: Prince Myshkin, who features as a beautiful Christ-like figure in Dostoevsky's notebooks, or the merchant's son Rogozhin. More concretely this means she must either forgive herself for her fall and accept the Prince's unexpected offer of marriage or she may refuse to forgive herself and run away with Rogozhin. Overwhelmed by the Prince's proposal, she initially accepts, but that same evening, ostensibly to 'save' the Prince from ruin, she runs away with Rogozhin. Then she returns to the Prince and runs away again. Finally, Nastasya Filippovna offers to cede the Prince to Aglaya Epanchina—a magnanimous yet self-centred gesture (she wants praise and acceptance in exchange). When Aglaya spurns her offer, Nastasya Filippovna claims the Prince for herself—only to run away to Rogozhin for a third time, this time to death at his hands. Nastasya Filippovna's self-hatred wins, and the consequences are dire for all: Nastasya is killed by Rogozhin; the Prince returns to a state of idiocy; Rogozhin gets sent to prison; and Aglaya, against the wishes of her family, marries an émigré pretending to be a Polish count. Evil thus triumphs over good, and Nastasya's beautiful, iconic portrait becomes a lie—a form of formlessness.

Dostoevsky's famous use of the words 'evil' or 'good' to indicate a text's metaphysical dimension is found in his earlier work, *Notes from Underground*. There, as we have seen in the discussion of double-voicedness in Chapter 3, Dostoevsky had already used the word for 'evil' (*zlo*) to move the action to the metaphysical sphere. The novel's second sentence—'I am a spiteful man'—can also be translated 'I am an evil man.' Activating the concept of evil this early forces readers to re-evaluate the novel's seemingly straightforward opening line, 'I am a sick man', which can be read literally, figuratively, or both. However, as I suggest in Chapter 3 on freedom and polyphony, Dostoevsky also links the concepts of good and evil to the concepts of free will and choice. The underground man chooses to represent himself as sick, evil, and unattractive, yet he does so defensively, always looking over his shoulder at potential readers, trying to keep us off-guard so that we will buy his premises and conclusions. Like the third-person narrator of *The Idiot*, the first-person narrator of *Notes from Underground* thus dramatizes an internal struggle between egoism and altruism, which James Scanlan identifies as the two poles of Dostoevsky's ethical thinking. In these works and elsewhere, wilful perversion prevails over intuitive kindness.

Self-assertion versus self-surrender

Throughout his writing, the writer increasingly identified Christ as his moral ideal. By 1864, following the death of his first wife Maria Isaeva, Dostoevsky pens a famous reflection linking moral goodness to beauty through the figure of Christ:

> To love someone *as oneself*, in accordance with Christ's commandments, is impossible. The law of personality [*zakon lichnosti*] is binding on earth. The *self* stands in the way. Christ alone could do it, but Christ was an eternal ideal, toward which man strives and must strive, by the law of nature. Meanwhile, after the appearance of Christ, as *the ideal of man in the flesh*, it became as clear as day that the development of personality should come to this (at the very end of development, at the very point of attaining the goal): that the person should find, should recognize, should with the full force of his nature be convinced, that the highest use someone can make of his personality, of the full development of his *self*, is to annihilate this *self*, as it were—to give it totally to each and everyone, undividedly and unselfishly. And this is the greatest happiness. In this way the law of the *self* merges with the law of humanism, and, in merging, the two—both the *self* and the *all* (seemingly two extreme opposites)—are mutually annihilated for each other, while at the very same time each separate person attains the highest goal of his individual development.
>
> (16 April 1864 Notebook entry; Scanlan translation)

The key ideas here are anti-Romantic—not glorification of the individual self but subordination of the individual to the collective, 'for everyone'. These are ideas that continue throughout Dostoevsky's work and culminate in his 1880 speech in honour of Alexander Pushkin, Russia's great poet. Dostoevsky sees evil in the assertion of self, of ego, and 'the ideal' in the voluntary surrender of ego for the benefit of 'everyone'. As is fitting for a Christian thinker, Dostoevsky's aesthetics locates the individual as a member of the Russian Orthodox community, an identity that is both personal and communal.

As Jackson points out, Dostoevsky uses the word *obraz* to establish the close connection between ethics and aesthetics. The word *obraz* means not only 'form' or 'image' but 'icon'. The Bible says that humans are created in the image (*obraz*) and likeness of God. In this view, any turning away from the image of God—that is, from the good, from a moral response—is a deformation. Dostoevsky saw this turning away in the workings of pride, that is, in the assertion of ego. As seen above, Dostoevsky attributes free will to humans: we are free either to assert ourselves or to subordinate ourselves to something greater. This Dostoevskian theme continues throughout his work and is particularly highlighted in Ivan Karamazov's 'Legend of the Grand Inquisitor' (discussed both in Chapter 3 on freedom and polyphony and in Chapter 6 on eternal questions). Evil, as seen in spite and malice, is an assertion of self and thus a perversion or deformation of the image of God within us. The underground man models this kind of perverted ego assertion for Dostoevsky's readers. Consequently, when Dostoevsky uses the adjectives for 'good' and 'evil', he is signalling not just a moral category, but an aesthetic one as well.

Readers of *The Idiot* witness Nastasya Filippovna's internal struggle as a struggle between good and evil. Full of compassion, the Prince is moved by Nastasya's moral suffering. Rogozhin, by contrast, is moved by her physical beauty. Myshkin sees through Nastasya's experience-hardened exterior to the insecure, trustful, child within. He tries to act for her benefit. Rogozhin desires only to possess her; he acts for his own benefit. Nastasya Filippovna vacillates between these two men, as she vacillates between her self-images. Will she choose the Prince or Rogozhin—forgiveness, acceptance, and resurrection or unforgiveness, self-hatred, and death?

In a critical scene at the Ivolgins', Nastasya Filippovna, responding to the Prince's rebuke—'And aren't you ashamed of yourself?'—turns to Mme Ivolgina and apologizes for her rudeness: 'he's right, I'm not like that' (Pt I, ch. 10). She thus acknowledges her moral core, accepts the rebuke, and asks for forgiveness—a humbling of self that confirms her moral goodness. This frequently overlooked scene thus demonstrates the power of the penetrative word; the Prince reminds Nastasya Filippovna of her manners and her moral self. His rebuke gets her to change her behaviour and apologize, a rare moment in the novel.

As Nastasya Filippovna wavers between her self-images, she frequently lacerates herself in her desire to sacrifice herself for the sake of the Prince. We see this when she throws the Prince over at her name-day party and runs away with Rogozhin, but also later when she wants to relinquish the Prince to Aglaya Epanchina. Unfortunately, both Aglaya and Nastasya desire to save the Prince from each other, so their actions and words are full of ego. Nastasya wants recognition for her sacrifice; Aglaya wants recognition as Myshkin's saviour. Aglaya does not perceive Nastasya as a self-sacrificer but as a rival. Both women's desire for recognition wins out, to disastrous effect for all.

Two kinds of beauty

This scene of rivalry asks readers to differentiate between physical and moral beauty. Both Nastasya Filippovna and Aglaya are known for their beauty, but when they meet they do not display their moral beauty, the kind of beauty that the Prince reportedly says will 'save the world' (Bk III, ch. 5). The phrase 'beauty will save the world' has engendered its own history, living on as a t-shirt motto or tattoo, and most often it is attributed to Dostoevsky the author or to Prince Myshkin. In the novel, the Prince never confirms that he is its source; it rather originates with Kolya Ivolgin, Ganya's younger brother (Bk III, ch. 5).

Dostoevsky ensures that readers pay attention to the phrase by having Ippolit, a young nihilist dying of tuberculosis, repeat it three times in one paragraph. At the Prince's birthday party in Pavlovsk on his host Lebedev's porch, Ippolit first draws attention to this enigmatic statement by asking the Prince to confirm that he had said that beauty will save the world. Moving from enquiry to affirmation, Ippolit next proclaims loudly to the assembled guests that the Prince had declared that beauty will save the world and that he had done so because he was in love (without naming Aglaya). Finally Ippolit asks what kind of beauty will save the world, leaving Dostoevsky's readers to speculate about beauty and what kind of beauty has the capacity to save the world. If we apply this statement to Nastasya's meeting with Aglaya, it is clear that the Prince's putative statement refers not to physical but to moral beauty.

Demons: an intergenerational drama

The Idiot is often seen as Dostoevsky's most sustained treatise on beauty, with its portrayal of Prince Myshkin as a Christ-like figure linking beauty to morality. Dostoevsky's next novel, *Demons*, highlights beauty and places it in the context of an intergenerational struggle of fathers vs children. Both novels focus on the physical and moral beauty of particular characters. In *The Idiot*, the narrator draws attention to both the physical and moral beauty (or lack thereof) of Nastasya Filippovna, Aglaya Epanchina, and Prince Myshkin, and the moral goodness/beauty of Mme Epanchina and Mme Ivolgina. In *Demons*, characters comment on Liza Tushina's and Stavrogin's physical beauty, but not without reservations. Stavrogin's beauty is unnatural and disturbing; he appears to be wearing a mask, and, as we learn, he lacks a moral centre. Like Stavrogin, Liza can be capricious. In *Demons*, the meek—Mme Stavrogina's ward Dasha Shatova and the bible peddler Sophia Matveevna (Ulitina)—are commended for their moral beauty.

The two most powerful passages linking the beautiful and the good in *Demons* are Stepan Trofimovich Verkhovensky's speech in defence of beauty at the fundraising fete for the provincial governesses and his deathbed confession. Strikingly, Stepan Trofimovich starts his speech at the fete by invoking the need for universal forgiveness: 'Messieurs, the last word in this matter is all-forgiveness' (Pt III, ch. 1.4). As we see in *The Idiot*, forgiveness offers a method of healing, of integrating parts of self, of bringing individuals together in some kind of concord. In appealing to universal forgiveness, Stepan Trofimovich is attempting to end the generational conflict that plagues Russia. To proclaim all-forgiveness is to declare oneself on the side of unity, of bringing people together despite their differences. In this spirit, Stepan Trofimovich acknowledges the enthusiasm and idealism of the younger generation. Nonetheless, he feels that the younger generation has gone astray by declaring the 'replacement of one beauty with another' (Pt III, ch. 1.4).

Here Stepan Trofimovich directly cites the contemporary debate about utilitarian ethics, when he declares that

> Shakespeare and Raphael are of higher value than the
> emancipation of the peasants, of higher value than the national
> principle, of higher value than socialism, of higher value than the
> younger generation, of higher value than chemistry, of higher
> value than almost all humankind, for they are already the fruit,
> the real fruit of humankind, and perhaps the highest fruit there
> can possibly be! The ultimate form of beauty has already been
> achieved, and without that achievement I would perhaps not
> agree to go on living… (Pt III, ch. 1.4)

Stepan Trofimovich thus rejects the utilitarian view of beauty proposed by the nihilists, who professed an amalgam of materialism, utilitarianism, scientism, and atheism. He engages with the 1860s debate between the fathers, the generation of the 1840s who grew up on the idealist views of Saint-Simon, Fourier,

Fathers and children

In *Demons* and other works, Dostoevsky participates in an ongoing literary conversation about generational conflict in Russia between 'men of the forties' and 'men of the sixties'. Stepan Trofimovich Verkhovensky, with his idealism, abstract intellectualizing, and Romantic world-view, represents the educated elite of the 1840s ('fathers'). The typical representative of this generation studied in Western Europe, where he imbibed liberal political and philosophical ideas which could never be implemented, or even expressed openly, under Nicholas I's repressive regime. Alexander II, who took the throne in 1855, emancipated the serfs in 1861 and initiated sweeping reforms at all levels of society, including the judicial system, higher education, and the press. The younger generation ('sons') took full advantage of these new freedoms, leaving behind the moderate liberalism of their fathers and embracing radical and revolutionary programmes of action. Ivan Turgenev's 1861 novel *Fathers and Children* (or *Fathers and Sons*) served as the most visible expression of this generational conflict for readers of the time. Dostoevsky lampoons Turgenev in *Demons* in the figure of the effete writer Karmazinov. Many members of the younger generation in Dostoevsky's novel are either tutored by Stepan or fall under his influence in various ways. In this way their excesses, and the catastrophes that befall their town, are shown to originate in Stepan's liberal, Western, 1840s, forms of thinking.

Box credit: Carol Apollonio

and Georges Sand, and their nihilist children—the generation of the 1860s. But Dostoevsky raises the stakes. By aligning Stepan Trofimovich's son Peter Verkhovensky with the devil and forces of division, Dostoevsky raises the generational battle to the metaphysical level. By this point in the novel, Peter Verkhovensky has broken with his father and revealed his fully divisive character.

Initially described as a man with a forked tongue, Peter continually uses language to deceive, humiliate, and confuse.

Peter's aesthetic views mark him as a youth gone astray. He conceives a plan to sow division throughout Russia by creating an idol, a Pretender. He calls Stavrogin 'a beauty!' and declares, 'I love beauty. I'm a nihilist, but I love beauty. Do nihilists really not love beauty? It's only idols they don't love; well I love idols! You are my idol!...You are a leader, you are the sun, and I am your worm...' (Pt II, ch. 8). Here we see a false beauty. Stavrogin may be beautiful, but the narrator has revealed that it is an artificial beauty: 'he seems to be a perfect beauty, but at the same time also repulsive. They say his face recalls a mask' (Pt I, ch. 2.1). Peter's proposal to sow division throughout Russia by revealing Stavrogin to the masses as a Pretender further cements the view of him as an agent of the demonic. Furthermore, by calling Stavrogin a Pretender, he draws on Russia's fragmented past, when pretender tsars divided the land, creating political unrest and fomenting rebellions.

He declares that his plan will succeed because of Stavrogin's beauty and indifference: 'you're a beauty, proud as a god, seeking nothing for yourself, surrounded with an aureole of self-sacrifice, and "in hiding." The main thing is the legend! You'll conquer them, all you need do is look at them, and you'll conquer them' (Pt II, ch. 8). Stavrogin's wife, the holy fool Marya Lebyadkina, on the other hand, sees through Stavrogin's mask and accuses him of being a pretender: 'You look a lot like him, a lot...Only mine is a bright falcon and a prince...Get away, you impostor!' (Pt II, ch. 2).

Finally, Peter murders the former conspirator Shatov to unite his followers; he has the Lebyadkins murdered so that he can blackmail Stavrogin and free him to marry Liza Tushina. He also persuades Liza to abandon her fiancé and her fixed life and delivers her to Stavrogin. Like the biblical devil, Peter tries to bind his interlocutor with promises—power, freedom, sexual licence. Moreover, while he claims to be acting on behalf of a larger organization, all his actions are taken to consolidate his own power and position and to avenge perceived past wrongs.

By having Stepan Trofimovich propose both a concept of all-forgiveness and a concept of moral beauty as the highest non-material achievements of humankind, Dostoevsky keeps the argument on the metaphysical plane. He also links this early speech with Stepan's culminating, deathbed confession. Peter's call to divide and conquer thus works antithetically to his father's call for all-forgiveness, a refrain Stepan reprises at novel's end. On his deathbed, Stepan asks the bible peddler Sophia Matveevna to read to him the passage about Jesus exorcising the Gadarene swine and then identifies himself as a force of division:

> That's us, us, and them, and my son Petrusha...et les *autres avec lui*, and I perhaps am the first, standing at the very head; and we shall throw ourselves, the madmen and the possessed, from a rock into the sea and we shall all drown, and that's no more than we deserve...But the sick man [Russia] will be healed and 'will sit at the feet of Jesus'. (Pt III, ch. 7.2)

Here at last Stepan thus moves away from his earlier feverish declaration that 'one can correct the mistakes' in the Bible—'that remarkable book' (Pt III, ch. 7.2). As he lies dying, Stepan finally accepts responsibility for his own sins and proclaims, 'Oh, let us forgive, let us forgive, let us first of all forgive everyone everywhere...We will hope that they will forgive us as well. Yes, because each and every one of us is guilty as far as others are concerned. We are all guilty!' (Pt III, ch. 7.2). This move towards universal forgiveness is necessary because all humans contain the spark of the divine, which forms a core of moral beauty:

> The whole law of humankind's existence consists in the fact that man has always been able to bow before the immensely great. If you

deprive people of the immensely great, they will cease to live and
die in despair. The immeasurable and infinite are as necessary to a
person as that small planet on which he lives...Every person,
whoever he is, needs to bow down before the Great Idea! Even the
most stupid person needs something great. Petrusha...Oh how
I yearn to see them all again! They don't know, they don't know that
this same eternal Great Idea is contained within them!

(Pt III, ch. 7.3)

The critical idea here is that all humans contain a spark of the
eternal within; all are God's creatures. In this novel of
intergenerational conflict, Dostoevsky thus pits father against son,
forgiveness against murder, obeying the divine within rather than
turning away from it. Two kinds of beauty form the linchpin of the
argument: true, moral beauty, the glow of the heavenly within
each individual, and false, immoral beauty, an outward
appearance rather than an internal essence.

Two kinds of beauty: *The Brothers Karamazov*

Stepan Trofimovich's discourse about beauty thus prepares the
way for Dmitry Karamazov's perspective on the existence of two
kinds of beauty. Dmitry speaks of the discord in the human heart
as a battle between two ideals, the ideal of the Madonna and the
ideal of Sodom. He asks, 'Can there be beauty in Sodom? Believe
me, for the vast majority of people, that's just where beauty
lies—did you know that secret? The terrible thing is that beauty is
not only fearful but mysterious. Here the devil is struggling with
God, and the battlefield is the human heart' (Bk III, ch. 3). In
identifying beauty in Sodom here, Dmitry thus separates the
moral from the aesthetic, which accounts for the discord in his
heart. For Dostoevsky, the two cannot be separated.

Stepan Trofimovich's discourse on moral beauty in *Demons* also
argues for forgiveness, thus paving the way for the elder Zosima
and Dmitry Karamazov in *The Brothers Karamazov* to profess the

responsibility of each for all. Both Dmitry and young Zosima (Zinovy) were army officers. Each was tempted away from moral action by externals; each was directed back to God by a blow of fate. Each in turn professes responsibility not only for his own actions but for those of others.

Zosima's turning point comes when he provokes an unnecessary duel. He returns home and in a fit of anger strikes his orderly Afanasy in the face so hard that he draws blood. The next morning he has an epiphany and realizes, 'each of us is truly guilty before everyone and for everyone, only people do not know it, and if they knew it, the world would at once become paradise' (Bk VI, ch. 2c). He throws himself at Afanasy's feet and asks forgiveness—a step to reintegrating himself, dispelling his inner discord. After allowing his opponent to fire a shot, Zinovy asks for his forgiveness, an act which is unacceptable to his fellow officers until he declares that he is going to join a monastery. Unlike Dmitry, who sees the ideal of Sodom as part of human nature, Zosima declares, 'Paradise...is hidden in each one of us, it is concealed within me, too, right now, and if I wish, it will come for me in reality, tomorrow even, and for the rest of my life' (Bk VI, ch. 2d). Zosima thus asserts that suffering comes from disunity and isolation from others, and he sees forgiveness as a step towards unity and community.

Dmitry's turning point occurs after he is arrested and interrogated for the death of his father. When Alyosha visits him in prison, Dmitry accepts responsibility for all, citing his dream of a burned-out village with homeless women standing outside, one of whom has a cold, starving child crying for warmth and food. He explains to Alyosha that he will accept his punishment for the sake of the 'little children' (*dityo*):

> It's for the 'little children' that I will go. Because everyone is guilty for everyone else. For all the 'little children', because everyone is guilty for everyone else. For all the 'little children', because there are

little children and big children. All people are 'little children'. And
I'll go for all of them, because there must be someone who will go
for all of them.   (Bk XI, ch. 4)

Just as Zosima sees forgiveness as a step towards unity and
community, Dmitry sees taking responsibility for suffering in
the world as a means of expiating his sins and rejoining
community. Dmitry's concern for children also connects him to
his half-brother Ivan and to Dostoevsky himself.

By having Dmitry take a position that so nearly resembles that of
the holy elder Zosima, Dostoevsky reinforces our sense of Dmitry's
moral goodness. Even though Zosima's vision encompasses all of
nature and all of humankind, whereas Dmitry's focuses on human
community, both see beyond themselves to their place in the
larger world. More significantly, Dostoevsky has both Zosima and
Dmitry, in their own ways, follow the path of Christ through
taking responsibility for others, which means acknowledging
communal bonds based on the presence of the sacred within each
person. Each sees a future manifested in the new life they have
committed themselves to live. By linking their moral visions to
Christ, whom Dostoevsky sees as a repository of beauty,
Dostoevsky thus unites their aesthetic and ethical visions.

Chapter 6
Eternal questions: *The Brothers Karamazov*

When most people think of Dostoevsky, they think of him in terms of significant metaphysical questions such as good and evil or the existence of God. They do so with good reason, for Dostoevsky not only dramatized these questions in his work, he struggled with them throughout his life—his religious doubts contending with his faith in God. Early in his life, Dostoevsky wrote that he was 'a child of this century, a child of disbelief and doubt', and that he had always been and would ever be. Yet he believed that God sent him moments of profound faith which led him

> to believe that there is nothing more beautiful, more profound,
> more sympathetic, more reasonable, more courageous, and more
> perfect than Christ…More than that, if someone succeeded in
> proving to me that Christ was outside the truth, and, if truth really
> were outside Christ, I would rather remain with Christ than with
> the truth.   (Omsk, 15 February 1854)

The idea in this early letter informed Dostoevsky's writing and his poetics, that is, his rhetorical and narrative strategies. He professes allegiance to faith over reason, but more importantly, allegiance to embodied truth. By acknowledging allegiance to the incarnate Christ, Dostoevsky rejects abstract and rationalized thought. Instead, he devotes himself to the concrete, the embodied—to life in all its richness, life thoroughly embedded in social relations. As a result, even though Dostoevsky understands the philosophical implications of human actions, he dramatizes them with characters and images rather than theorizing about them. This chapter will focus on *The Brothers Karamazov* and will explore in particular how the two younger brothers—the intellectual Ivan and the gentle, spiritual Alyosha—wrestle with the eternal questions by tackling the issue of Christ—the incarnate God.

Faith and morality

In a pivotal conversation in the local tavern, Ivan identifies 'the eternal questions' for his brother Alyosha: 'Is there a God, is there immortality?' (Bk V, ch. 3). These questions are linked because Dostoevsky held that belief in God is the source of morality. He thus repudiated the atheism of the radical critics, seeing socialism and anarchism as the eternal questions 'from the other end' (Bk V, ch. 3), man-centred rather than God-centred. In *Demons*, the nihilist Kirillov dies by suicide to prove the primacy of man, citing the need for a man-God; in *The Adolescent*, socialists discuss the man-God; in *DW*'s ongoing polemic on suicide, Dostoevsky repeatedly argues that belief in God binds humans to the earth; and in *The Brothers Karamazov*, Ivan articulates Dostoevsky's belief most strongly—without belief in God and immortality, there is no morality, 'all is permitted'.

The theme of belief in God is explicitly raised in Book III, chapter 8 of *The Brothers Karamazov*, when Fyodor Karamazov, a buffoonish doubter, asks his sons Ivan and Alyosha whether God and immortality exist. He receives opposing answers. Ivan insists that neither exist; Alyosha affirms that both do. This conversation prepares for the brothers' meeting in the tavern where Ivan tests Alyosha by citing a litany of episodes of child abuse that he has collected from the newspapers. After the third story, about a landowner who had his dogs hunt down and rip apart a serf boy who had accidentally injured his favourite hunting dog, Ivan asks

Alyosha how to respond to the landowner. Alyosha's initially replies 'Shoot him!'—the response Ivan has been waiting for. Alyosha then asks Ivan why he is testing him, and Ivan replies, 'I won't give you up to your [elder] Zosima' (Bk V, ch. 4), that is, to the monastic life and all that it entails.

Theodicy and the suffering of children

Ivan confesses that he wrestles with theodicy—'with my pathetic, earthly Euclidean mind, I know only that there is suffering, that none are to blame', yet he wants retribution: 'I am a believer. But then there are the children, and what am I going to do about

Theodicy, the Book of Job, and *The Brothers Karamazov*

The Brothers Karamazov offers a sustained and profound treatment of the problem of theodicy—the existence of evil and suffering in a world where God is both all-good and all-powerful. The Book of Job—the Old Testament's great theodicy—figures centrally in the novel. Like Zosima, who was profoundly moved at the age of 8 when he heard the Book of Job read in church, Dostoevsky first encountered the story in childhood, in an adaptation of Bible stories that was his household reading. In 1875 Dostoevsky was rereading the Book of Job, and recorded thoughts about it in his notebooks for *The Adolescent* and *The Brothers Karamazov*. Sending off Book V, 'Pro and Contra', including 'The Grand Inquisitor', to his editor, he wrote of his concern that Ivan's 'blasphemous' vision would be persuasive to the younger generation. He promised that the next instalment (Book VI) would provide an answer through the story of Zosima's death and deathbed conversations—not a sermon, but an artistic vision of a real, tangible Christianity—and claimed that it was for the sake of this, Zosima's book, that he had written the entire novel.

Box credit: Carol Apollonio

them? That is the question I cannot resolve' (Bk V, ch. 4). Ivan renounces a higher harmony based on the tears of even one small child:

> I want to forgive, I want to embrace, I don't want more suffering. And if the suffering of children goes to make up the sum of suffering needed to buy truth, then I assert beforehand that the whole of truth is not worth such a price. I do not, finally, want the mother to embrace the tormentor who let his dogs tear her son to pieces! She dare not forgive him! Let her forgive him for herself, if she wants to, let her forgive the tormentor her immeasurable maternal suffering; but she has no right to forgive the suffering of her child who was torn to pieces, she dare not forgive the tormentor, even if the child were to forgive him! And if that is so, if they dare not forgive, then where is the harmony? Is there in the whole world a being who could and would have the right to forgive?...I'd rather remain with my unrequited suffering and my indignation, even if I am wrong. Besides they have put too high a price on harmony; we can't afford to pay so much for admission. And therefore I hasten to return my ticket.... It's not that I don't accept God, Alyosha, I just most respectfully return my ticket.   (Bk V, ch. 4)

This speech highlights the themes of forgiveness and of children's suffering that run throughout Dostoevsky's work. By coupling children's suffering with forgiveness, and by repeating the active verb 'forgive' (nine times) and the word 'suffering' (six times) in this passage, Ivan intensifies his appeal to Alyosha's sympathy both cognitively and emotionally. Likewise, Dostoevsky intensifies reader response to Ivan's speech. We are equally moved by examples of child abuse and understand how difficult it is to forgive abusers.

After calling Ivan's rant a 'rebellion', Alyosha answers Ivan's question about who has the right to forgive such abuse by citing Christ, who 'can forgive everything, forgive all and for all, because he himself gave his innocent blood for all and for everything'

(Bk V, ch. 4). This conversation introduces Ivan's legend of the Grand Inquisitor, a fictional figure who rejects God's world and offers people 'miracle, mystery, and authority' instead of the freedom Christ offers. Ivan's story ends with the silent Christ kissing the Grand Inquisitor on his 'bloodless' lips, a story that not only affirms Christ's right to forgive all sinners, but demonstrates that he can and does forgive even the Grand Inquisitor's apostasy. By then plagiarizing Christ's action and kissing Ivan, Alyosha follows Christ's example—he may not approve of his brother's apostasy, but he accepts Ivan despite his rebellion against God and his world. Since the kiss 'originates in Ivan's sensibility', Alyosha may in fact 'be sowing in Ivan the seed of his own redemption', leaving us to ask, with Robin Feuer Miller, who is saving whom?

Temptation, retribution, and forgiveness

By imitating Ivan's Christ, Alyosha takes his stand on the question of forgiveness, but the question of divine justice returns to haunt him when the elder Zosima dies. Instead of the expected miracle of odourless bones, the elder's body stinks in the heat. Alyosha is crushed—he had expected a miracle, but the narrator notes, 'it was not miracles that he needed, but only "a higher justice"' (Bk VII, ch. 2), adding, 'Where was Providence and its finger?' (Bk VII, ch. 2). His envious friend, the cynical seminarian Rakitin, finds the grief-stricken Alyosha lying on the ground and accuses him of rebelling against God. Recalling his conversation with Ivan, Alyosha replies, 'I do not rebel against my God, I simply "do not accept his world"' (Bk VII, ch. 2). Rakitin seizes upon Alyosha's response as an opportunity to cause a good man to fall. Yet unbeknownst to Rakitin, Dostoevsky draws a parodic parallel between his creation Rakitin and Ivan's creation the Grand Inquisitor. Whereas Ivan's Inquisitor uses elevated language to tempt Christ with miracle, mystery, and authority, Rakitin basely tempts Alyosha with sausage, vodka, and a visit to Grushenka (the fallen woman who is the object of Fyodor and the eldest son Dmitry's rivalry). Alyosha's initial agreement to all three temptations emphasizes that his spiritual dilemma lies between earthly forgiveness and retribution. The problem of divine justice still haunts him.

Alyosha is saved from all three temptations both by his grief at Zosima's death and by Grushenka's compassion. Although Grushenka had promised her cousin Rakitin 30 roubles for bringing Alyosha to her, once she hears that Alyosha's beloved elder has just died, she jumps off Alyosha's lap and treats him as a sister would. Then she confesses her original intention to seduce Alyosha. Grushenka also confesses her current dilemma—whether to forgive or to seek retribution on the man who had seduced her five years earlier. The question of forgiveness or retribution, raised by Ivan in the tavern, thus hovers in the air as Grushenka heads off to Mokroye to meet her former lover. Fortified by Grushenka's sisterly love, Alyosha returns to the monastery, seeking inspiration for his desire to embrace Christ-like forgiveness.

In the monastery, Father Paissy is reading from the Gospel of John about Christ's first miracle at the wedding at Cana, where he turns water into wine. As Paul Contino points out, Alyosha dreams that he is there in Cana—where he witnesses Christ both immanent at the wedding and transcendent at a heavenly banquet to which all are invited. He also sees Zosima both in his coffin and as a participant in the wedding feast—simultaneously dead to this world and alive in the next. Moreover, this dream is both solitary and communal. Alyosha is by himself, but he is with others at a heavenly feast, presided over by the incarnate Christ. Significantly, Christ's first miracle, performed in Cana at his mother's behest, is an ordinary one—thus recalling the small miracle of Grushenka's sisterly compassion for Alyosha.

Following his dream, Alyosha rushes outside to commune with the earth and the sky, where he falls weeping to the earth and feels the urge 'to forgive everyone and for everything and to ask forgiveness, oh, not for himself! but for all and for everything'

(Bk VII, ch. 4). In this scene, which aligns more with the elder's representation of a positive and loving faith than with mainstream Orthodoxy, Dostoevsky here stresses the theme of forgiveness, which has been associated with Christ even before Ivan shares his story of the Grand Inquisitor, where Christ is the source of all-forgiveness. Alyosha thus chooses the path of Christ and of his elder Zosima—the path of universal forgiveness, rather than the path of pride and retribution chosen by Ivan and his Inquisitor. Consequently, Alyosha rises from the ground 'a fighter, steadfast for the rest of his life', remembering, 'someone visited my soul in that hour' (Bk VII, ch. 4). Alyosha's good memory links him to his half-brother Dmitry, who confesses that someone visited his soul while he was crouched under his father's window—a presence that saved him from striking his father with the pestle in his hand.

The Grand Inquisitor, the Russian monk, and the devil incarnate

Although Alyosha is the audience for Ivan's Legend of the Grand Inquisitor, he is also witness and scribe of Zosima's last words. In this way, Dostoevsky uses Zosima and his discourses in 'The Russian Monk' (Bk VI) as a response to 'The Grand Inquisitor' (Bk V, ch. 5). Instead of the Grand Inquisitor's ambitious pride, Zosima preaches humility. Instead of alienation from the masses, Zosima preaches the interconnection of all living things. Instead of human manipulation of miracle, mystery, and authority, Zosima preaches the mystery and miracle of creation. Instead of the few taking on the sins of the many, Zosima preaches each taking responsibility for all. Instead of rejecting Christ, Zosima embraces Christ as a kenotic model of self-giving love. Instead of the power of the few over the many, Zosima preaches universal love for all living things. Instead of judging others, Zosima reminds us that we cannot judge others without judging ourselves. Instead of demanding retribution, Zosima warns us to fear it. Instead of material pleasure, Zosima preaches spiritual joy. Despite these refutations, Dostoevsky feared that 'The Russian Monk' would fail to undercut Ivan's Inquisitor, so he included other ways of doing so.

Dostoevsky primarily undercuts the Inquisitor by parody—he portrays Rakitin as a materialist tempting Alyosha, and he describes the youth Kolya Krasotkin, in Book X, 'The Boys', as an imperious Inquisitor compelling the young children in his care to complete obedience. Dostoevsky also circles back to mention the Inquisitor in Ivan's nightmare in Book XI. There, in a serious-comic vein, he creates a double for Ivan, an incarnate devil whose relationship to Ivan resonates with the novel's questions about the Christian incarnation. Although Ivan professes not to believe in God and immortality, he actually vacillates between belief and unbelief—an ambivalence identified early in the novel by Zosima. In his monastery cell, Zosima declares to Ivan that if the question of God and immortality 'cannot be resolved in a positive direction, then it will never be resolved negatively either—for you know this quality of your heart; therein lies the whole of its torment' (Bk II, ch. 6). This eternal question of God's existence thus haunts Ivan, as it does the entire novel.

Book XI chronicles Ivan's visits to Smerdyakov, the probable unacknowledged fourth brother, spawn of Fyodor Karamazov and the holy fool Lizaveta Smerdyashaya. In their three meetings, Ivan, who has acted as Alyosha's tempter, and whose Grand Inquisitor tells the story of Christ's temptations by the devil in the wilderness, now himself becomes the tempted. Smerdyakov, a literalist deaf to Ivan's ambivalences and doubts, tries to convince Ivan that he, rather than Smerdyakov, is the real murderer of Fyodor Pavlovich. At their third meeting, after hearing his repulsive half-brother confess to the murder, Ivan vows to expose him in court the next day and to take responsibility for leading him astray. Instead of going directly to the police, however, he returns home and has a nightmare in which the devil appears to him.

Ivan's devil, like Ivan's father, is a shabby sponger around 50 years old, a punster who specializes in dirty tricks, and an exhibitionist liar. In creating this devil, Dostoevsky not only links son to father, he plunges readers into Ivan's soul, exposing his ethical and metaphysical anxieties. Ivan acknowledges his devil as a manifestation of his shame—'the embodiment of myself, but only one side of me... of my thoughts and feelings, but only the most loathsome and stupid of them' (Bk XI, ch. 9). Ivan's devil invokes the incarnate Word of God, claiming that he was an eyewitness to Christ's ascent into heaven, and keeps readers focused on the question of incarnation by telling tales of his own incarnation and its woes.

He torments Ivan, confronting him with the question of whether or not he, the devil, exists: 'after all, who knows whether proof of the devil is also proof of God' (Bk XI, ch. 9). By constantly questioning his own reality, the devil foregrounds Ivan's metaphysical doubts and the novel's theme of belief. The devil also declares, 'like you, I myself suffer from the fantastic, and that is why I love your earthly realism' (Bk XI, ch. 9). By creating a fantastic yet realistic devil, Dostoevsky brings metaphysics down to earth.

Recounting his incarnational anecdotes, the devil dwells on the literal to explain the metaphysical. He therefore complains of catching cold while materializing in the 'ether' in order to attend a cocktail party on earth, accentuating his physical symptoms to explain the suffering caused by his alienation. He also claims to have been cured by Hoff's extract, a dubious remedy that was regarded as quackery in its own day, one that clearly cannot cure his underlying ailment—alienation from God. The devil's comic efforts to publish a thank-you note to Hoff, the eponym of the questionable elixir, demonstrate his desire to alleviate his metaphysical alienation with acceptance by the human community. Contemporary journals refuse to print the devil's letter on the grounds that he does not exist. With this episode, Dostoevsky takes a jab at Russian censorship, and his devil comically reminds Ivan and readers about the question of belief: the atheist editors of progressive journals do not believe in the devil, just as they do not believe in God. The devil thus returns readers to the theme that has been alive from the very beginning of the novel.

Ivan's devil next proposes an even more extreme physical cure for his alienation when he declares: 'My dream is to become incarnated, definitively, irreversibly, as some fat 250-pound merchant's wife and to believe everything that she believes. My ideal is to go to church and light a candle from a pure heart, by God. That would be the end of my suffering' (Bk XI, ch. 9). Readers may well ask why Dostoevsky has Ivan—a Russian intellectual suffering from radical ideas, shame of origins, and existential angst—manufacture a devil who posits this startling ideal. This goes to the heart of how Dostoevsky tackles the question of incarnation—seriously yet comically. If we take the devil to be a figure of metaphysical and social alienation, we can see his desire to become a female believer as an alienated male's longing for authenticity and belonging. Most importantly, however, the image raises questions about bodies, especially about incarnation, which lies at the heart of Dostoevsky's Christological poetics.

By creating a devil who thematizes incarnation, Dostoevsky highlights the paradox at the heart of Christianity. First, as the devil explores aspects of his physical life on earth, Dostoevsky evokes Christ—the incarnate Word of God. Bearing in mind that Christ as Logos combines word and image, we see how the incarnate Christ conjoins Dostoevsky's theodicy with his literary practice. Second, the devil demonstrates how Christ's incarnation haunts Ivan. As the devil says,

I was there when the Word who died on the cross was ascending into heaven, carrying on his bosom the soul of the thief who was crucified to the right of him; I heard the joyful squeals of the cherubim singing and shouting 'hosanna', and the thundering shout of rapture from the seraphim, which made heaven and all creation shake. And I swear by all that's holy, I wanted to join the chorus and cry out 'hosanna!' with everyone else.   (Bk XI, ch. 9)

Here the devil not only invokes Christ as 'Word' or Logos from John's Gospel, he also spells out the incarnational plot propelling the Gospels: Christ's descent to earth in human form followed by his ascent to heaven. By including the thief from the Gospel of Luke in his ascension story, the devil invokes the two concepts that haunt Ivan—belief and forgiveness. By conjuring up a comic chorus of joyful cherubim and seraphim, the devil underscores the theme of belief.

As he tells tales of his own incarnation, the devil leads us to forget that he is a mental construct—a product of Ivan's unconscious. By proposing his semi-comic incarnational ideal, Ivan's devil stresses the material aspects of embodiment. By asserting eyewitness status at Christ's death and resurrection, the devil authenticates his own existence. The devil's mention of the cherubim and their hosanna also reminds readers of Ivan's brother Alyosha, whom both Grushenka and Dmitry call a cherubim—a noun that can be either singular or plural in Church Slavonic. Ivan's devil thus deploys Dostoevsky's rhetorical strategy of both/and, another blurring of boundaries that mimics the duality of incarnation and therefore of Christ.

Ivan's devil not only reveals that Ivan has Christ on the brain, he also reminds Ivan of both Alyosha and the divine power of forgiveness. Ivan's nightmare thus echoes the meeting of the two brothers in the tavern, where Ivan plays the devil and tempts Alyosha, who then reminds him of the all-forgiving Christ. There Ivan deftly achieves his goal—setting himself up to tell his Legend of the Grand Inquisitor, which, as Alyosha points out, actually praises Christ. In both cases, the tempter (Ivan/his devil) reminds the tempted (Alyosha/Ivan) of Christ, thereby demonstrating awareness of his alienation from humankind as well as the path back to God.

Hosanna

In the story of the ascension, Ivan's devil uses the word 'hosanna', which early Christians used to praise God and Christ. Dostoevsky uses the word 'hosanna' to signify belief. In his notebooks for *The Brothers Karamazov*, for instance, he writes about the Grand Inquisitor:

> In Europe there are not and *have not been expressions* of atheism of such power. Accordingly, it is not as a boy that I believe in Christ and preach him, rather my *hosanna* has passed through a great *crucible of doubts*, as the devil says in that same novel of mine.
>
> (*Notebook* for 1881, 27:86)

As this declaration shows, Dostoevsky understood the Inquisitor's significance for his polemic on atheism. It also illustrates how Dostoevsky places serious metaphysical claims in the mouths of semi-comic characters like Ivan's devil.

In *The Brothers Karamazov*, the devil notes that

> Without criticism, there would be only 'hosanna'. But for life it is not enough to have only 'hosanna', it is necessary that this 'hosanna' pass through the crucible of doubt, and so forth, in the same vein ... for suffering is life. Without suffering, what pleasure would there be in it—everything would turn into an endless prayer service: it would be holy, but a bit dull. (Bk XI, ch. 9)

Through the devil's words, Dostoevsky outlines three phases of belief: (1) 'only "hosanna"', corresponding to naive faith, perhaps that of merchants' wives; (2) 'hosanna' undergoing trial in the crucible of doubt, here presumably Ivan's doubts about Christ; and (3) 'hosanna' that has passed through the crucible of doubt, presumably mature faith, such as Dostoevsky's. Malcolm Jones observes that 'any reading of [Dostoevsky's] religious thought that focuses primarily on his "hosanna" will detach it from the spiritual and intellectual travail that gave it birth, and therefore from its most characteristic and most modern features'.

Ivan's devil associates hosanna with the cherubim, an angelic community of joyous believers, which he contrasts with his own isolated and alienated singularity, that which makes him the devil but also a modern. Dostoevsky not only writes against the tradition of representing the devil as a grand figure, he has Ivan internalize his devil, another sign of his modernity. Ivan's devil also posits suffering as a corollary of consciousness, the ascendancy of mind over heart. Recalling Zosima's claim that great suffering arises from the lack of self-respect and the inability to love (Bk II, ch. 2), we may see the devil as a dialectician pointing Ivan back to community.

Ivan's devil also reminds him of another legend Ivan had written earlier, proof that Ivan had 'hosanna' on the brain for at least seven years before writing the Legend of the Grand Inquisitor. In his earlier legend, an atheist philosopher dies. Upon waking to discover an afterlife, he angrily lies down in protest for almost 1,000 years before rising and walking the quadrillion kilometres necessary to reach heaven's gates. When he arrives, however, he immediately proclaims that for the sake of his first two seconds in paradise, he would walk a quadrillion quadrillion kilometres raised to the quadrillionth power. As the devil observes, 'In a word, he sang "hosanna"...' (Bk XI, ch. 9). In this early story, Ivan dramatizes how conviction conflicts with experience in the head and heart of a Russian 'thinker and philosopher'. Significantly, at the outset, the atheist philosopher clings stubbornly to his intellectual convictions in the face of an experience contradicting them. In Ivan's next story, the Grand Inquisitor does the same. Ivan's atheist philosopher rejects God and the afterlife from intellectual conviction but eventually he converts. Ivan's Inquisitor, on the other hand, initially believes but eventually succumbs to the temptation of pride. The Grand Inquisitor challenges Christ, that is, God the son, and his decision to give freedom to humankind. But with Christ's kiss burning in his heart, the Inquisitor releases Christ: his worldly power bows to the kenotic power of the incarnated Christ.

Kenosis

The Incarnation thus serves as a stumbling block to Ivan. Ivan, who sees himself as a creator, would rather identify with the powerful Inquisitor than the humiliated Christ. In the Christian tradition, incarnation not only involves embodiment, but kenosis, a self-giving love that expresses itself in self-emptying: Jesus 'emptied himself, taking the form of a slave, being born in human likeness. And being found in human form, he humbled himself by becoming obedient to death—even death on a cross!' (Phil. 2:7). In taking human form, Christ divests himself of traditionally expressed attributes of divine power. By extension, this act confers freedom on humankind, particularly the wherewithal to choose a relationship with God. Ivan portrays his Grand Inquisitor as an individual who wilfully rejects God the Father and God the son. He elevates himself, arguing that freedom serves as a burden rather than a gift to humankind. Yet Ivan's legend pits the cardinal's satanic pride against the kenotic Christ's self-giving love. Just as the devil in Ivan's nightmare bears witness to Ivan's intellectual struggles, so Christ's presence in Ivan's story evidences the great struggle within his heart. As Alyosha watches over Ivan, he perspicuously observes, 'God, in whom he did not believe, and his truth were overcoming his heart, which still did not want to submit' (Bk XI, ch. 10). Alyosha thus identifies his brother's internal struggle as part of a metaphysical process.

In the end, the two brothers do not represent opposite ends of a spectrum. Rather, the spectrum runs from Alyosha at one end to Smerdyakov at the other. Alyosha is a believer, a follower of the kenotic Christ, and a disciple of his spiritual father Zosima. Smerdyakov is a literalist and unbeliever, and a murderer of his purported earthly father. Ivan is a doubter, a man who desperately longs to believe in God and the forgiveness offered by Christ. Dostoevsky thus places Ivan in the middle. Ivan's and Alyosha's dreams both feature Christ and reveal much about their unconscious: Alyosha dreams of Christ at the wedding feast of Cana; Ivan dreams of a devil, who questions his own existence yet who reminds Ivan that he has Christ, the solution to his unbelief, on the brain. Alyosha ends the novel as a leader of a band of boys, calling upon them to cherish their childhood memories. Ivan ends the novel unconscious, but his dream/nightmare of the devil gives readers hope that he will recover and eventually embrace the Christ he has himself imagined in his poem.

Dostoevsky thus tackles the eternal questions of good and evil and the existence of God and lays out his Christological poetics in concrete ways. Zosima's biography in 'The Russian Monk' (Book VI) introduces the example of a good man, Zosima's older brother Markel. Markel, who proclaimed that each of us is guilty before everyone and everything (Bk VI, ch. 2), can serve as a model and inspiration to others, just as Christ can serve as a model and inspiration for all. Dmitry, innocent of the murder of his father, bears this message in the novel when he is convicted and sentenced to Siberian prison, thereby taking on his brothers' guilt. Zosima's teachings follow Christ's model of self-emptying love, acceptance of responsibility for all, belief in the interconnectedness of all on earth and in other worlds, beyond our ken. They thus offer readers a guide to living in a world filled with suffering by holding a belief in a good God, a Christ figure of self-abnegation and love of others. The figure of Job connects Zosima, who praises him, and Ivan, who wrestles with the same question of evil in the world. But it is Ivan's devil, who torments Ivan in a comic vein, who reveals Dostoevsky's Christological poetics. Throughout his meeting with Ivan, the devil serves as a double, mirroring Ivan's doubts and reflecting his longing to belong to a community of believers. He comically reduces the metaphysical to the literal, yet keeps the metaphysical issues

7. Dostoevsky in 1879.

alive. Most importantly, the devil demonstrates that Ivan has Christ on the brain—an image he cannot renounce, a means of escape from his self-enclosure and alienation. For Christ preaches universal love and forgiveness, and in those two virtues, Dostoevsky sees the salvation of the world (see Figure 7).

Chronology

1821	Fyodor Mikhailovich Dostoevsky is born, the second of seven children, on 30 October to Mikhail Andreevich and Maria Fyodorovna Dostoevsky at the Mariinsky Hospital for the poor, where his father was a doctor.
1834-7	Attends Chermak Private Boarding school in Moscow.
1837	Dostoevsky enrols in the St Petersburg Academy of Engineers; his mother dies.
1839	Father dies under dubious circumstances; some claim he was murdered by the peasants on his small property near Tula.
1841	Dostoevsky completes his course at the Academy, is promoted to officer status, and begins officer training.
1843-4	Service as a military engineer in St Petersburg.
1844	Resigns his military service to devote all his energy to writing. First publication is a translation of Balzac's 1833 novel *Eugénie Grandet* into Russian.
1846	First novel, *Poor Folk*, is published to acclaim and Dostoevsky enters St Petersburg literary circles. His second novel, *The Double*, is received with considerably less enthusiasm.
1847-9	Several works published, including 'White Nights' and 'The Landlady'. Dostoevsky is diagnosed with epilepsy. Revolutions break out in Western Europe. He joins a discussion circle led by the utopian socialist Mikhail Butashevich-Petrashevsky, and becomes a member of a secret radical society within that circle that aims to publish incendiary pamphlets.

1849	Dostoevsky works on the unfinished novel *Netochka Nezvanova*. With others in the Petrashevsky Circle, he is arrested and imprisoned for eight months in solitary confinement in the Peter and Paul Fortress. On 22 December he and several others are led out to Semyonovsky Square; the prisoners are read a death sentence, which they learn at the last moment has been commuted to penal servitude in Siberia.
1850–4	Imprisoned at the Omsk fortress in Siberia. His almost exclusive reading during this period is the *New Testament*.
1854	After serving his four-year prison term Dostoevsky is sent to serve as a soldier in Semipalatinsk.
1855	Nicholas I dies and is succeeded by Alexander II, who will initiate a series of liberal reforms. Dostoevsky is now able to exchange letters.
1857	Marries Maria Dmitrievna Isaeva in Kuznetsk. 'The Little Hero', a story written in prison in 1849, is published.
1858	Writes *The Village of Stepanchikovo and its Inhabitants* and *Uncle's Dream*.
1859	Gains the right to return to St Petersburg, where he will be under police surveillance.
1861	Establishes, with his elder brother Mikhail, the journal *Time* (*Vremya*), in which are published his fictionalized prison memoir, *Notes from the Dead House*, the novel *The Insulted and Injured*, and numerous articles elucidating his 'native soil' (*pochvennichestvo*) agenda. On 19 February the serfs are emancipated.
1862	First trip to Western Europe (England, France, Germany, Italy, and Switzerland). Dostoevsky acquires a debilitating gambling habit abroad.
1863	Publishes travel notes, *Winter Notes on Summer Impressions*, expressing a critical view of European politics, economics, and culture. Government censors close down *Time*. Second trip to Europe, where he pursues an affair with the young writer Apollonaria Suslova.

1864	The Dostoevsky brothers establish a second journal, *Epoch* (*Epokha*), in which *Notes from Underground* is published. Dostoevsky's wife Maria dies from tuberculosis, leaving her son in his care. Mikhail Dostoevsky dies, leaving Dostoevsky with crushing debts.
1865	*Epoch* collapses. Dostoevsky goes to Europe, where he gambles.
1866	*Crime and Punishment* is serialized monthly through the year in Mikhail Katkov's *The Russian Herald*. In October Dostoevsky hires a 20-year-old stenographer, Anna Grigorievna Snitkina, to whom he dictates the novel *The Gambler*, completing it within a month, meeting a contract deadline and thereby retaining the copyrights to his published works—present, past, and future.
1867	Dostoevsky marries Anna and they escape financial ruin by travelling to Europe (Geneva, Florence, and Dresden), where they will live for the next four years.
1868	Daughter Sonya is born in Geneva, but dies there at the age of three months. *The Idiot* begins serial publication in *The Russian Herald*.
1869	Daughter Liubov is born in Dresden. Dostoevsky begins writing *Demons*.
1870	*The Eternal Husband*.
1871–2	Serial publication of *Demons*. The Dostoevsky family returns to St Petersburg. Son Fyodor is born.
1873	Dostoevsky edits *The Citizen* (*Grazhdanin*), a conservative weekly, in which he writes a popular column called 'The Diary of a Writer'.
1875	*The Adolescent* is published serially in the liberal journal *Fatherland Notes*. Son Alexei is born.
1876	Dostoevsky begins publishing *The Diary of a Writer* as a separate monthly periodical. He buys a house in Staraya Russa.
1877	Dostoevsky begins writing *The Brothers Karamazov*.
1878	3-year-old son Alexei dies suddenly. Dostoevsky visits an elder, Amvrosy, at the Optina Pustyn monastery, incorporating details from this encounter in the novel.

1879	*The Brothers Karamazov* begins serial publication.
1880	Dostoevsky delivers his famous speech at the opening of the Pushkin monument in Moscow.
1881	On 28 January Dostoevsky dies from a lung haemorrhage in St Petersburg and is buried in the cemetery of the Alexander Nevsky monastery.

Dostoevsky

References

Chapter 1: Dostoevsky's dramatic life and writing: *Notes from the Dead House* and the *Diary of a Writer*

All citations of Dostoevsky's writings are taken from F. M. Dostoevskii, *Polnoe sobranie sochinenii v tridtsati tomakh* (Akademia nauk, 1972–90). All citations are indicated by volume and page number. Volume 1, pages 186–7 will be written (1:186–7). All translations are my own, unless otherwise indicated.

Chapter 2: Duality and doubles: *The Double*

Jillian Porter, *Economies of Feeling: Russian Literature under Nicholas I* (Northwestern University Press, 2017), 89–106. I owe most of the observations about Russian currency in this chapter to Porter.

On 'rational egoism' and the intellectual culture of the time, see James Scanlan, *Dostoevsky the Thinker* (Cornell University Press, 2002), 57–80.

On suicide in Dostoevsky's works, see Amy D. Ronner, *Dostoevsky as Suicidologist: Self-Destruction and the Creative Process* (Lexington Books, 2020).

Chapter 3: Freedom and polyphony: *Notes from Underground*

Olga Meerson, 'Old Testament Lamentation in the Underground Man's Monologue: A Refutation of the Existentialist Reading of

Notes from Underground', *Slavic and East European Journal*, 36, 3
(1992): 317–22. Here p. 319.

Robert L. Belknap, 'The Unrepentant Confession', in *Russianness*, ed.
Robert L. Belknap (Ardis, 1990), 113–23, p. 122.

For scripting, see Sarah Young, *Dostoevsky's* The Idiot *and the Ethical
Foundations of Narrative: Reading, Narrating, Scripting* (Anthem
Press, 2004).

Chapter 4: Space, social justice, and scandal: *Crime and Punishment*

I owe the observations about the ambiguity of Petersburg's topography in
Crime and Punishment to Boris Tikhomirov's *'Lazar'! Gryadi von':
Roman F. M. Dostoevskogo 'Prestuplenie i nakazanie' v sovremennom
prochtenii* (Sererbryani vek, 2005), especially pp. 197 and 302.

On the connections between the two Lazaruses, see Linda Ivanits,
Dostoevsky and the Russian People (Cambridge University Press,
2008), 62–3, 74–5.

On the 'threshold', see Mikhail Bakhtin, *Problems of Dostoevsky's
Poetics*, ed. and trans. Caryl Emerson (University of Minnesota
Press, 1984), 61, 170.

Chapter 5: Aesthetics and ethics: *The Idiot* and *Demons*

The opening statement about the ancient Greek conception of *kalon*
comes from Paul Contino, *Dostoevsky's Incarnational Realism:
Finding Christ among the Karamazovs* (Cascade Books, 2020),
240, fn. 87.

Robert L. Jackson, *Dostoevsky's Quest for Form: A Study of His
Philosophy of Art* (Yale University Press, 1966), 1–11.

James Scanlan identifies egoism and altruism as the two poles of
Dostoevsky's ethical thinking. Scanlan, *Dostoevsky the
Thinker*, 81–117.

The quotes from *Demons* in this chapter are taken, with minor
adjustments, from Fyodor Dostoyevsky, *Demons*, trans.
Robert A. Maguire, ed. Ronald Meyer (Penguin Books, 2008).

Chapter 6: Eternal questions: *The Brothers Karamazov*

Robin Feuer Miller, *The Brothers Karamazov: Worlds of the Novel*
(Yale University Press, 2008), 70.

On theodicy, see Gary Rosenshield, 'Dostoevskii and the Book of Job: Theodicy and Theophany in *The Brothers Karamazov*', *Slavic and East European Journal*, 60, 4 (2016): 609–32.

Paul Contino, *Dostoevsky's Incarnational Realism: Finding Christ among the Karamazovs* (Cascade Books, 2020), 114.

Malcolm V. Jones, *Dostoevsky and the Dynamics of Religious Experience* (Anthem Press, 2005), 26.

Further reading

Chapter 1: Dostoevsky's dramatic life and writing: *Notes from the Dead House* and the *Diary of a Writer*

The most comprehensive biography of Dostoevsky in English is Joseph Frank's five-volume *Dostoevsky* (Princeton University Press): *The Seeds of Revolt, 1821–1849* (1976); *The Years of Ordeal, 1850–1859* (1983); *The Stir of Liberation, 1860–1865* (1986); *The Miraculous Years, 1865–1871* (1995); and *The Mantle of the Prophet, 1871–1881* (2002). A one-volume abridged version of this set, *Dostoevsky: A Writer in his Time*, came out in 2012.

For information about the journalistic culture of Dostoevsky's time, see Deborah A. Martinsen, ed., *Literary Journals in Imperial Russia*. Studies of the Harriman Institute. Cambridge Studies in Russian Literature (Cambridge University Press, 1997).

On the *Diary of a Writer*, see Gary Saul Morson, *The Boundaries of Genre: Dostoevsky's* Diary of a Writer *and the Traditions of Literary Utopia* (Northwestern University Press, 1988).

On *pochvennichestvo* and on the connection of Dostoevsky's journalism to his fiction, see Ellen Chances, 'Dostoevsky's Journalism and Fiction', in *Dostoevsky in Context*, ed. Deborah A. Martinsen and Olga Maiorova (Cambridge University Press, 2015), 272–9. See also Ellen Chances, 'Literary Criticism and the Ideology of *Pochvennichestvo* in Dostoevsky's Thick Journals, *Vremia* and *Epokha*', *Russian Review*, 34, 2 (1975): 151–64.

Susanne Fusso offers a detailed analysis of Dostoevsky's important interactions with the editor Mikhail Katkov in her *Editing Turgenev, Dostoevsky, and Tolstoy: Mikhail Katkov and the Great Russian Novel* (Northern Illinois University Press, 2017), 137–56.

For Dostoevsky's gambling, see Richard Rosenthal, 'Gambling', in *Dostoevsky in Context*, ed. Deborah A. Martinsen and Olga Maiorova (Cambridge University Press, 2015), 148–56. This book features 35 valuable essays on the social, cultural, and political context in which Dostoevsky wrote.

See Linda Ivanits, *Dostoevsky and the Russian People* (Cambridge University Press, 2002) for an excellent study of the common people, and the alienation of the educated classes from the Russian soil, in Dostoevsky's work.

On the theme of suicide in Dostoevsky's writing, see Amy D. Ronner, *Dostoevsky as Suicidologist: Self-Destruction and the Creative Process* (Lexington Books, 2020).

Robin Feuer Miller discusses patterns of conversion in Dostoevsky's work in her *Dostoevsky's Unfinished Journey* (Yale University Press, 2007), 105–27.

Chapter 2: Duality and doubles: *The Double*

On the phenomenon of doubling in Dostoevsky's works, see Roger B. Anderson, *Dostoevsky: Myths of Duality* (University of Florida Press, 1986).

Jillian Porter, *Economies of Feeling: Russian Literature under Nicholas I* (Northwestern University Press, 2017), 89–106, situated Dostoevsky and other 19th-century Russian writers within the changing economic culture of their time.

James Scanlan, *Dostoevsky the Thinker* (Cornell University Press, 2002), 57–80, addresses the intellectual context of Dostoevsky's writing. His chapter on *Notes from Underground* is a must-read for the philosophically minded.

On the gothic in Dostoevsky's works, see Katherine Bowers, *Writing Fear: Russian Realism and the Gothic* (University of Toronto Press, 2022).

Chapter 3: Freedom and polyphony:
Notes from Underground

J. David Velleman, 'The Genesis of Shame', *Philosophy and Public Affairs*, 30, 1 (Winter 2001): 27–52, 35 is the most useful philosophical analysis of shame for my work on Dostoevsky.

Michael Andre Bernstein, *Bitter Carnival: Ressentiment and the Abject Hero* (Princeton University Press, 1992), 87–120.

Olga Meerson, 'Old Testament Lamentation in the Underground Man's Monologue: A Refutation of the Existentialist Reading of *Notes from Underground*', *Slavic and East European Journal*, 36, 3 (1992): 317–22.

For more on how Dostoevsky uses pronouns in *Notes from Underground*, see Carol Apollonio, 'I Gotta be Мы': The Plot of the Egotistical Pronoun in Dostoevsky's *Notes from Underground*, *Dostoevsky Monographs*, 5 (2016): 23–35.

Robert L. Belknap, 'The Unrepentant Confession', in *Russianness*, ed. Robert L. Belknap (Ardis, 1990), 113–23, 122.

On the philosophical and literary context of Dostoevsky's treatment of inertia and free will, see Liza Knapp, *The Annihilation of Inertia: Dostoevsky and Metaphysics* (Northwestern University Press, 1996), 15–43.

Robert Jackson offers seminal readings of the workings of egoism and faith in Dostoevsky's *Notes from Underground*, *Notes from the Dead House*, and other works in his *The Art of Dostoevsky: Deliriums and Nocturnes* (Princeton University Press, 1981).

On the censored religious passages in *Notes from Underground*, see Carol Flath, 'Fear of Faith: The Hidden Religious Message of *Notes from Underground*', *Slavic and East European Journal*, 37, 4 (1993): 510–29.

Dostoevsky had a lifelong polemic with Rousseau and his *Confessions*. For more on that polemic, see Robin Feuer Miller, *Dostoevsky's Unfinished Journey* (Yale University Press, 2007), 86–104. See also Miller's 'Dostoevsky and Rousseau: The Morality of Confession Reconsidered', in *Dostoevsky: New Perspectives*, ed. Robert L. Jackson (Prentice Hall, 1984), 82–98.

On questions of law, see Richard H. Weisberg, *The Failure of the Word: The Protagonist as Lawyer in Modern Fiction* (Yale University Press, 1999), 192–261.

On duelling, see Irina Reyfman, *Ritualized Violence Russian Style: The Duel in Russian Culture and Literature* (Stanford University Press, 1999), 192–261.

Chapter 4: Space, social justice, and scandal: *Crime and Punishment*

Deborah A. Martinsen's *Crime and Punishment: A Reader's Guide* (Academic Studies Press, 2022) offers a concise and engaging introduction to the novel's structure and themes.

For a broader treatment of Petersburg, social justice, and Western literary influences, see Donald Fanger, *Dostoevsky and Romantic Realism: A Study of Dostoevsky in Relation to Balzac, Dickens, and Gogol* (The University of Chicago Press, 1967).

On the visual composition of the novel, see Roger Anderson's 'The Optics of Narration: Visual Composition in *Crime and Punishment*', in *Russian Narrative and Visual Art: Varieties of Seeing*, ed. Roger Anderson and Paul Debreczeny (University of Florida Press, 1994), 78–100.

On gender issues in Dostoevsky's time as addressed in *Crime and Punishment*, see Barbara Engel, 'The "Woman Question," Women's Work, Women's Options', in *Dostoevsky in Context*, ed. Deborah A. Martinsen and Olga Maiorova (Cambridge University Press, 2015), 58–65, esp. 59.

For the 'threshold', see Mikhail Bakhtin, *Problems of Dostoevsky's Poetics*, ed. and trans. Caryl Emerson (University of Minnesota Press, 1984).

On shame, see Deborah A. Martinsen, *Surprised by Shame: Dostoevsky's Liars and Narrative Exposure* (The Ohio State University Press, 2003).

On the poetics of accusation and confession in Dostoevsky's works, see Carol Apollonio, *Dostoevsky's Secrets* (Northwestern University Press, 2009).

On geography and space, see Anne Lounsbery, *Life is Elsewhere: Symbolic Geography in the Russian Provinces, 1800–1917* (Northern Illinois University Press, 2019).

Chapter 5: Aesthetics and ethics: *The Idiot* and *Demons*

For Dostoevsky's aesthetics and ethics, see Robert L. Jackson, *Dostoevsky's Quest for Form: A Study of His Philosophy of Art* (Yale University Press, 1966).

Chapter 6: Eternal questions: *The Brothers Karamazov*

Robin Feuer Miller, *The Brothers Karamazov: Worlds of the Novel* (Yale University Press, 2008).

Paul Contino, *Dostoevsky's Incarnational Realism: Finding Christ among the Karamazovs* (Cascade Books, 2020).

Vladimir Kantor, 'Pavel Smerdyakov and Ivan Karamazov: The Problem of Temptation', in *Dostoevsky and the Christian Tradition*, ed. George Pattison and Diane Oenning Thompson (Cambridge University Press, 2001), 189–225.

Malcolm V. Jones, *Dostoevsky and the Dynamics of Religious Experience* (Anthem Press, 2005).

Index

For the benefit of digital users, indexed terms that span two pages (e.g., 52–53) may, on occasion, appear on only one of those pages.

COMMUNISM
A Very Short Introduction
Leslie Holmes

The collapse of communism was one of the most defining
moments of the twentieth century. At its peak, more than a
third of the world's population had lived under communist
power. What is communism? Where did the idea come from
and what attracted people to it? What is the future for
communism? This Very Short Introduction considers these
questions and more in the search to explore and understand
communism. Explaining the theory behind its ideology, and
examining the history and mindset behind its political,
economic and social structures, Leslie Holmes examines the
highs and lows of communist power and its future in today's
world.

www.oup.com/vsi

EXISTENTIALISM
A Very Short Introduction
Thomas Flynn

Existentialism was one of the leading philosophical movements of the twentieth century. Focusing on its seven leading figures, Sartre, Nietzsche, Heidegger, Kierkegaard, de Beauvoir, Merleau-Ponty and Camus, this *Very Short Introduction* provides a clear account of the key themes of the movement which emphasized individuality, free will, and personal responsibility in the modern world. Drawing in the movement's varied relationships with the arts, humanism, and politics, this book clarifies the philosophy and original meaning of 'existentialism' - which has tended to be obscured by misappropriation. Placing it in its historical context, Thomas Flynn also highlights how existentialism is still relevant to us today.

www.oup.com/vsi

GERMAN PHILOSOPHY
A Very Short Introduction
Andrew Bowie

German Philosophy: A Very Short Introduction discusses the
idea that German philosophy forms one of the most revealing
responses to the problems of 'modernity'. The rise of the modern
natural sciences and the related decline of religion raises a
series of questions, which recur throughout German philosophy,
concerning the relationships between knowledge and faith,
reason and emotion, and scientific, ethical, and artistic ways
of seeing the world. There are also many significant philosophers
who are generally neglected in most existing English-language
treatments of German philosophy, which tend to concentrate
on the canonical figures. This *Very Short Introduction* will include
reference to these thinkers and suggests how they can be
used to question more familiar German philosophical thought.

www.oup.com/vsi

GLOBAL ECONOMIC HISTORY
A Very Short Introduction
Robert C. Allen

Why are some countries rich and others poor? In 1500, the income differences were small, but they have grown dramatically since Columbus reached America. Since then, the interplay between geography, globalization, technological change, and economic policy has determined the wealth and poverty of nations. The industrial revolution was Britain's path breaking response to the challenge of globalization. Western Europe and North America joined Britain to form a club of rich nations by pursuing four polices: creating a national market by abolishing internal tariffs and investing in transportation, erecting an external tariff to protect their fledgling industries from British competition, banks to stabilize the currency and mobilize domestic savings for investment, and mass education to prepare people for industrial work.

Together these countries pioneered new technologies that have made them ever richer. Before the Industrial Revolution, most of the world's manufacturing was done in Asia, but industries from Casablanca to Canton were destroyed by western competition in the nineteenth century, and Asia was transformed into 'underdeveloped countries' specializing in agriculture. The spread of economic development has been slow since modern technology was invented to fit the needs of rich countries and is ill adapted to the economic and geographical conditions of poor countries. A few countries—Japan, Soviet Russia, South Korea, Taiwan, and perhaps China—have, nonetheless, caught up with the West through creative responses to the technological challenge and with Big Push industrialization that has achieved rapid growth through investment coordination. Whether other countries can emulate the success of East Asia is a challenge for the future.

www.oup.com/vsi

KIERKEGAARD
A Very Short Introduction
Patrick Gardiner

Søren Kierkegaard, one of the most original thinkers of the nineteenth century, wrote widely on religious, psychological, and literary themes.

This book shows how Kierkegaard developed his views in emphatic opposition to prevailing opinions. It describes his reaction to the ethical and religious theories of Kant and Hegel, and it also contrasts his position with doctrines advanced by thinkers like Feuerbach and Marx. Kierkegaard's seminal diagnosis of the human condition, which emphasizes the significance of individual choice, has arguably been his most striking philosophical legacy, particularly for the growth of existentialism. Both that and his arresting but paradoxical conception of religious belief are critically discussed by Patrick Gardiner who concludes this lucid introduction by showing how Kierkegaard has influenced contemporary thought.

'Marvellously lucid and readable book'

E. Pivcevic, University of Bristol

'Lucid sketch for the beginner of the thinking of the man who initially discarded theology for philosophy and literature, and subsequently influenced theology more.'

Theological Book Review

'Patrick Gardiner's beautifully written Kierkegaard makes him come alive both as a thinker and as a human being.'

Independent

www.oup.com/vsi

NIETZSCHE
A Very Short Introduction
Michael Tanner

The philosopher Friedrich Nietzsche was almost wholly neglected during his life, which came to an abrupt end on 25 August 1990. Since then he has been appropriated as an icon by an astonishingly diverse spectrum of people, whose interpretations of his thought range from the highly irrational to the firmly analytical.

Idiosyncratic and aphoristic, Nietzsche is always bracing and provocative, and temptingly easy to dip into. Michael Tanner's readable introduction to the philosopher's life and work examines the numerous ambiguities inherent in his writings. It also explodes the many misconceptions fostered in the hundred years since Nietzsche wrote, prophetically: 'Do not, above all, confound me with what I am not!'

'highly readable, an excellent introduction'

Guardian

www.oup.com/vsi

RUSSIAN LITERATURE
A Very Short Introduction
Catriona Kelly

Rather than a conventional chronology of Russian literature, Catriona Kelly's *Very Short Introduction* explores the place and importance of diverse literature in Russian culture. How and when did a Russian national literature come into being? What shaped its creation? How have the Russians regarded their literary language? At the centre of the web is the figure of Pushkin, 'the Russian Shakespeare', whose work influenced all Russian writers, whether poets or novelists, and many great artists in other areas as well.

'brilliant and original, taking an unexpected approach to the subject, and written with great confidence and clarity.'

Peter France, University of Edinburgh

'a great pleasure to read. It is a sophisticated, erudite, searching, and subtle piece of work. It is written in a lively and stimulating manner, and displays a range to which few of Dr Kelly's peers in the field of Russian scholarship can aspire.'

Phil Cavendish, School of Slavonic and East European Studies, University of London

THE SOVIET UNION
A Very Short Introduction
Stephen Lovell

Almost twenty years after the Soviet Unions' end, what are we to make of its existence? Was it a heroic experiment, an unmitigated disaster, or a viable if flawed response to the modern world? Taking a fresh approach to the study of the Soviet Union, this Very Short Introduction blends political history with an investigation into the society and culture at the time. Stephen Lovell examines aspects of patriotism, political violence, poverty, and ideology; and provides answers to some of the big questions about the Soviet experience.

www.oup.com/vsi